Peering through a Mist

A Mom's Journey in Loss and God's Grace

Janet Lindsey

WESTBOW
P R E S S
A DIVISION OF THOMAS NELSON

Unless otherwise noted, Scripture was taken from the
Holy Bible, New International Version.
Copyright © 1973, 1978, 1984 by International Bible Society. Used by permission of Zondervan Publishing House. All rights reserved.

Scripture also was taken from The Message. Copyright © 1993, 1994, 1995, 1996, 2000, 2001, 2002, 2005 by NavPress Publishing Group.

Scripture noted with "KJV" was taken from the King James Version of the Bible.

WestBow Press books may be ordered through booksellers or by contacting:

WestBow Press
A Division of Thomas Nelson
1663 Liberty Drive
Bloomington, IN 47403
www.westbowpress.com
1-(866) 928-1240

ISBN: 978-1-4497-3612-5 (sc)
ISBN: 978-1-4497-3613-2 (hc)
ISBN: 978-1-4497-3611-8 (e)
Library of Congress Control Number: 2011963685
Printed in the United States of America
WestBow Press rev. date: 1/23/2012

In loving memory of Gary Scott Lindsey.

We don't yet see things clearly. We're squinting in a fog, peering through a mist. But it won't be long before the weather clears and the sun shines bright! We'll see it all then, see it all as clearly as God sees us, knowing him directly just as he knows us!

1 Corinthians 13:12, The Message

Contents

Acknowledgments

Thank you ...

To my husband, Ed, who is walking the heart-wrenching path with me. Thanks for understanding throughout the development of this book. Thank you for listening as I read, or commented, even though it made you cry. You are my soul mate. One day we will be with our son again.

To my parents, sisters, and sister-in-law, and their husbands, my nieces, and my mother-in-law. Your love and support toward us is continuous. I can't imagine going through this without you. You are grieving too, yet you care for us.

To our extended family and friends who have prayed, sent cards, visited us, fed us, and included us in your life. You have such kind hearts. We are truly grateful.

To our church family whose countless prayers are felt. Your acts of love and kindness will always be a reminder of what the body of Christ is about.

To Mark Rigsby, who proofread every page with expertise and knowledge and gave insight into making this book possible. I am thankful for your God-given gifts.

To Lynda Rizzardi, who proofread the book and made necessary corrections in grammar and punctuations. You are precious.

To my sister, Laura, whose computer knowledge far exceeds my own. Your talents and time were invaluable to completing this book. I love you and thank you.

To the thirty-three organizations who aided us in the search and recovery of our son. Without you, our son may have never been found. We thank you from our collective heart.

To Jesus, my Comforter and only Hope, the One to whom I hold fast. May You use my sorrow for Your purposes.

Preface

When our twenty-two-year-old son and only child died, our hopes and dreams for him and his future died. Our hopes of being grandparents vanished. We had devoted all those years in raising him and being a close family trio. When he was gone, the most important part of us died too, for he was our joy. We spent months in shock and disbelief.

Then the struggles of dealing with grief forced their way into our lives. We have endured sleepless nights and agonizing days. We have endured because God has poured His grace on us. He has given us the strength to get out of bed every day, even when we did not want to live. We have come to experience God in a different way. The God whose "thoughts are not your thoughts, neither are your ways my ways."[1] The God of Job. Though we do not understand and He has chosen not to answer our whys, He can still be trusted. He is sovereign. His ways and His thoughts are higher, deeper. He sees what we do not see. He has a purpose.

Romans 8:28 says, "And we know that in all things God works for the good of those who love him, who have been called according to his purpose." That doesn't mean He isn't going to allow afflictions, tragedies, sorrow, and even death. It simply means He will work things out for His purposes for spiritual and eternal good. This wasn't the verse I wanted quoted to me after our son's death. It was almost offensive to have someone quote this, as if everything would be all right after hearing that verse. My heartache now had the answer it desperately needed as to why this had happened! At that point in my grief, which was still shock and disbelief, quoting that verse did not help my heartache. It actually angered me. *How dare you tell me losing my only child is God working good,* I thought.

It would be another two years before I could swallow that verse and truly understand the meaning within. I cannot thank God for my son's tragic death, or in destruction from violent acts of nature, terminal illnesses, murders, abuse, hurt, and pain. These are the results of living in a sin-filled world. However, I can thank Him for the good works that develop from enduring these things. And I can thank Him for the grace and mercy He lavishes on us.

It is our response to afflictions where the good can work, and it is a choice. We can allow God to work in us, drawing us closer to Him, or we can blame Him, turning our backs in bitterness.

After the death of my husband's grandmother recently, my mother-in-law took her wigs to the local cancer center in the hope that it might have patients who needed them. An employee of the center noticed my mother-in-law's last name and asked if she knew my husband and me. When the connection was made, the employee asked if my mother-in-law was aware of how many people had given their lives to Christ because of Gary's death. She went on to explain that in her church, and other churches, there was evidence of this.

One young man came to the Lord at Gary's funeral.

That is fulfilling God's purposes. *That* is for spiritual and eternal good. *That* is the good working from a horrible tragedy.

I have come to a place where something good must come from losing him. Grief is too costly not to be used. There is urgency in my need. That is the purpose for writing and sharing my daily journals so that others may know they are not alone in their sorrow.

Our God is sympathetic and compassionate. He suffers with us. More than anything, there is hope, and it only comes through

Jesus. Because He lives, we will live, forever.[2] We will be with our loved ones again.

> In order to have a sympathetic God, we must have a suffering Savior, for true sympathy comes from understanding another person's hurt by suffering the same affliction. Therefore we cannot help others who suffer without paying a price ourselves, because afflictions are the cost we pay for our ability to sympathize. Those who wish to help others must first suffer.[3]

For "He who did not spare his own Son, but gave him up for us all"[4] surely understands my suffering and pain. I can rest assured in knowing my grief will end, and the mist will clear, when on that day I walk through the gateway and see Jesus and my son.

Chapter 1

Three Days, Three Nights

I was holding a coat in my arms when the news came that our son had been found. The next words I heard were, *"They're bringing him up now."* I buried my face in the coat. They were saying he drowned three days ago and they had just now found him. That moment, I wanted to die. Until then, I had hope, though it dwindled with each passing hour. Now there was no hope. My son's life was over. The finality of this truth was more than I could process at that moment. I was confused with what all this meant. What was I supposed to do, or was I to do anything? I felt helpless.

Grief can leave us with feelings of isolation and loneliness. No one's grief is the same. Most of us feel like no one understands our pain.

It took months before I could grasp the horrible reality that my son did not have a future here. He was gone. I was weak and felt I could not bear this heavy load of despair. I knew I must keep my eyes on the Lord but found this difficult. The God who allowed my hurt and pain was the same God who could tend to my every need.

I was angry at God. He seemed harsh and His way was hidden.

But I had a past with God, spending time in His Word and prayer, I knew His resources never ran out. This God, who had suffered too, would somehow help me. He is the Father of compassion, so He is able to comfort me.

This journey in grief has brought my faith to a different level. When we can honestly say from the depths of our souls—but even if He does not, we will still trust—we have journeyed far.

Gary Scott Lindsey. Twenty-two-year-old son of Ed and Janet Lindsey, an avid tournament bass angler who loved the outdoors and being on the water since he was a small boy. If he wasn't fishing, one could find him hunting deer in the woods.

Being good at both sports required skill. As a fisherman, he had learned moon phases, spawning, and habitats. He knew how to set a hook and lure them in because of dedicated practice. He won or placed in lots of fishing tournaments with his best friend, Jacob. They loved every minute on the water. Gary was also an experienced boater and excellent swimmer.

Gary was a Christian who regularly invited people to his church. He was full of life, with a charming personality, and was a pleasant person to be around. He had a beautiful smile and a big laugh that matched his smile. Gary was considerate and thoughtful, always seeing the good and positive qualities in others.

So on this day, as he had done so many times before, he hooked up his boat so that after work he could practice fishing for an upcoming tournament. It was Wednesday, April 8, 2009. He came to bid me good-bye and left for work. There were no warnings that my world would fall apart that day. It was the last time I saw my son alive.

I had a very hectic day at work, which made me anxious. Throughout the day, Gary called me several times just to talk. After work, I went to the grocery store. When I pulled into the parking lot, a strange sadness came over me. Not understanding why I felt that way, I found a more private spot out in the parking lot. I just sat there. I remember thinking, *Why do I feel this way?* I left without going into the store and headed home.

After I arrived home, Gary called again. This time, he told me he was breaking in a new boat for someone. It was an extremely windy day, and he said the water was rough. He assured me that he had worn a life jacket and a helmet all afternoon. He shared with me a change he was making in his life and some decisions he had made *that* day. I told him I was very proud of him for finally coming to that point and for making the right decisions.

At 5:33 p.m., as he was leaving work, he called me for the last time. He said he was going back to the lake to fish. I told him to be careful.

Then the sense of sadness that I felt in the grocery store parking lot began to creep back in. As I wondered why, my husband, Ed, came home. He was having these feelings too. I asked, "Why are we feeling this way?" He just shrugged his shoulders with little to say. Later, I left to go to Wednesday prayer meeting and music practice at church—even though on this night I really did not want to but felt obligated.

At 7:00, my phone vibrated. It was Ed. I wondered, *Why is he calling me when he knows I am at church?* I waited until church was over before I called him back.

"Is everything all right?" I asked.

"No," he said out of breath.

"What's wrong?" I asked.

"They found Gary's boat, but he is not in it."

My first thought was that he left his boat to go turkey hunting, since he had done that last week.

Ed said, "No, you don't understand. You need to get down here."

I could tell from his voice that things were not right. Over and over he tried to tell me where to meet him. However my mind wasn't processing; it was racing to solve the mystery of where Gary might be and what he was doing. I began gasping air.

Ed demanded, "Let me talk to somebody there."

"No, tell me again where to go," I replied.

"Have someone bring you," he said.

A lady from church drove me to the marina. My chest felt heavy. I thought, *God, what's happening? Please let him be okay.*

The drive down to the marina seemed like it took forever. The sweet lady tried to make conversation, but I could hardly think. I kept begging God to let Gary be all right.

The only other time I begged God for anything was twenty-three years before, and that was to have a child. After being told by a doctor that I may never have children, I was concerned it would never happen. Things changed when, only a few months after telling me that, I became pregnant, only to miscarry my child at three months. This left me devastated. It wasn't long until I learned I was pregnant again. We prayed nine months for that long-awaited child, Gary. Now, twenty-two years later, I was begging for that child's life.

As we approached, I saw all the rescue vehicles and the crowds that had gathered. My heavy breathing started again. We pulled into the lot, and Ed was there to meet me. I jumped out of the car, and he put his arm around me. Still trying to solve the problem, I said, "Ed, he's probably just turkey hunting and his boat got away from him."

But Ed said, "No, honey, his boat was still running on the bank."

"How do you know he's not on the bank somewhere?" I asked.

Ed replied, "Someone saw his boat in the water on the other side of the bridge, and there was no one in it."

The boat had a gas pedal and was still in gear, yet idling when they found it. There were no scratches or dents in the boat. Everything was in its proper place. The only thing unusual, was a thick plastic guide that holds the trolling motor in place, was broken at the base from the outside. There were no indications of a crash. Everything was there, but Gary.

"But …" I started to cry. *This isn't really happening. This is just a nightmare and I am going to wake up from it.*

His helmet and life jacket were still in the boat.

Soon, more rescue workers with vehicles and more friends arrived. The Red Cross came and brought coffee, blankets, and a tent for shelter. By now, it was dark and quickly getting colder. The water was only fifty-seven degrees. *Where was my son?* I pushed the thought of him in the cold, dark water out of mind. I refused to believe that was a possibility. He had to be on the bank somewhere and possibly hurt. Divers, sonar boats, police officers, firefighters, and, later, cadaver dogs all contributed to the rescue efforts. As word continued to spread, more and more of our church family arrived.

I knew I had to call my sister, Laura, before she found out from someone else. But what would I say? "Laura? Laura?" was all I could say.

"What's wrong?" she asked.

"They found Gary's boat, but they can't find Gary," I cried.

I told her we were at the marina.

"I'm coming," she said.

I was scared. I wanted my son so much that it hurt. Where was he? What happened? I had questions I kept asking, but no one could answer. "God, You know."

Someone estimated that over a thousand friends came to the marina to assist as the search continued into the night. And I kept asking questions. "Where was his boat?"

Ed pointed to the bank across the lake where the boat had come to rest.

I asked, "Has someone checked the bank or in the woods over there?"

Ed answered, "There are people searching the banks all along the lake and in the woods, but they haven't found anything."

"Who saw the empty boat?"

The rescue coordinator told me a man driving over the bridge looked down into the water and saw the empty boat slowly making large circles.

"What other information do we have?"

No more information.

"Did anyone see anything that might have happened?"

No, nothing.

"I need to know!" I asked the questions, but there were no answers.

My sister arrived with my niece, Loren. We hugged, and I could not answer their questions either. She called our sister, Rhonda, who lives in Alabama with her family. Immediately Rhonda and her daughter, Kristi were on their way.

"What about Momma and Daddy?" she asked.

Thinking we would have to tell them was sickening to me, but I knew we had to call before they found out from other sources. So Laura called, and they arrived with a friend who had driven them.

Daddy kept saying, "He's hurt on the bank somewhere. We need to find him! Is anyone searching the banks?"

"Yes, Daddy," I said.

We waited. Our pastor and his wife stayed with us into the early morning hours.

The rescue coordinator kept us informed of what was going on.

Then Rhonda and Kristi arrived. It was now 3:00 a.m. *Where is my son?*

Ed insisted I go home and try to rest. So Rhonda took me home, and I lay down for about an hour. It was 5:00 a.m. on Thursday, and I could not stand it any longer. I felt so far away from my son. Being at home for that short period of time made me anxious. *What if they find him and he needs me? What am I doing here? I need to get back to the marina.* I refused to think the worst, even though the thought kept trying to creep in. I knew that nothing was impossible with God and sought to dwell on that truth.

Gary had a new, modern GPS on his boat that recorded the boat's travels. The Tennessee Wildlife Resource Agency sent an expert from Nashville to help in the search. He used the data from Gary's GPS to follow the path Gary had traveled. They could tell where unusual moves began to occur. This apparently helped them know how to narrow their search.

Even more rescue crews arrived. More friends came and brought more food, drinks—anything they thought would help us. The Red Cross was still there with its provisions. Workers set up a tent to protect us from the dew at night and the sun during the day. Coffee and bottled water were available at all hours. Wednesday night had been cold, so they provided us with blankets. Not only were they meeting our physical needs, but their compassion was evident to us. They were willing to do anything for us. There were two chapters of the Red Cross who tended to our needs.

My heart was aching. I still asked questions that could not be answered. *Son, where are you?*

I went with some of my friends to search the banks along the lake. I could no longer stay in one place and do nothing. *He has to be somewhere,* I thought. *We just needed to find him, and soon.*

A local RV dealer sent a spacious RV for us to stay in during the day and night. Ed and his friend stayed during the night, even though they were busy helping with search-and-rescue efforts.

People were very generous and kind. Everyone just wanted to do something. Most could only wait and pray.

The divers dove all day. It was a slow process. The water was murky and cold, and the maximum vision was only about four feet. Gary's friends were out in their boats and using their depth finders.

Morning turned to afternoon, and all the ministers from our church arrived. One brought lunch for the crowd. Later, disaster-relief teams from area churches brought food.

My mind and heart were full. I am sure I walked around glassy-eyed. Despite not sleeping, Ed was going full force, helping the rescue people all he could. I hurt for him. I hurt for my parents.

Afternoon turned to night. We were constantly surrounded by friends, family, and the search-and-rescue teams.

Ed pulled me aside and said we needed to talk. He had just spoken privately with the person in charge of the operation, and I knew something was wrong. Ed said, "The situation doesn't look good."

I replied, "What do you mean? Have they found something?"

"No," he said. "I want you to understand that the longer we go without finding Gary, the more difficult it will be."

I bowed my head in thought. *Where is my son?*

I started praying. *God, You can do anything. You can show the search-and-rescue teams where to find Gary. If the worst has happened, and he is in the cold, dark water, You can place him on the bank, bring life back into his body, and no one would ever know but You. You can do that! If that is the horrible reality, please bring him back! I am begging, God, please.*

Night turned to early morning. Ed urged me to go home and try to rest. So again Rhonda took me home. When we arrived home, I sat on the floor of Gary's room and cried from the depths of my soul.

I hugged his dirty clothes. They still smelled like him and I ached for my son. I took his favorite sweatshirt, which he had worn the day before, to bed with me. I wanted to smell my son.

In the early morning hours of Friday, I slipped off to sleep. When I awoke, startled, I thought, *How could I sleep? My son is missing and I fell asleep!* I felt guilty even though I had been forty-eight hours without sleep. I had an urgency to get to the lake.

When we arrived back at the lake, it was 6:00 a.m. I was more distressed this day, remembering what Ed had told me the day before. Time was passing and we didn't seem any closer to finding

Gary. I was quiet and withdrawn, lost in my thoughts and agony. My prayers were pleas for Gary's life.

Our friends were so supportive. They came every day and offered food, prayers—anything that would comfort us. One friend brought me a plate of cookies. Another brought B12 vitamins so I would have strength. Others brought cakes, crackers, and bottles of water, and not just for us but for everyone who was there and waiting to hear news of Gary. I am not sure or even aware of what all these friends did for us and others, but their constant presence gave an overwhelming strength to us.

It was Friday morning and the weather report was not good. Heavy storms could move in later. This would not be good for the search. The wind could stir up the waters and change the path of everything. It would be like starting the search over.

A professional diver arrived and so did cadaver dogs. Helicopters arrived in the early afternoon to use infrared, invisible heat waves. This could detect a warm body from the banks and wooded areas.

We were continually informed what the search teams were doing. They narrowed the location of where they thought Gary was to within a hundred-yard radius. In a lake during a rescue mission, one hundred yards is huge.

The thought of him being under the cold, dark water was more than I could process. He was an excellent swimmer and boater. I didn't understand. I wanted answers. I was remembering all the group and private swimming lessons he had taken because I had a fear of water and did not want him to have the same fear. In the past, I refused to watch movies involving water because of this fear. *God, why water?*

He could swim! He was athletic and strong! I did not understand.

I wanted answers.

The dive team coordinator talked with us. He felt they were very close to finding him as long as the weather held and did not stir the waters. He was impressed with the two dogs that returned to the same spot and became overly excited each time. I wanted to pat these dogs. One, a Belgian Malinois named Rad, had odd eyes. He leaned against my leg and looked at me with those eyes. I felt like he knew where my son was.

One of the searchers found a shoe on the bank close to where they were running sonar. They brought the shoe to us to see if we recognized it. It was my son's! He always tied several knots in his laces and this was definitely his. "Oh, God, what happened?" I almost lost it. I wanted to keep the shoe, but it was needed for verification. When the shoe surfaced, reality that he might be in the water began finding its way into my heart. I could feel the hope I had been clinging to fading.

The weather continued to deteriorate. Tornado watches were announced so the search was postponed until the next day. It was only 4:00 p.m. The person in charge of the operation ordered everyone to leave. Ed insisted I go home. I did not want to, but knew they were evacuating the area. Ed had not slept since this whole nightmare started, and it was showing on his face. I wanted him to come home with me, but the rescue workers were continually asking him questions and needed him to be there. He was torn by what he should do: wanting to be with me but knowing it was imperative that he stay with the rescue workers. What would I do all afternoon and night at home not knowing anything? Ed planned to go to a local church with the rescue workers for safety from the storms.

Later, after I arrived home, I was standing in the front yard with my dogs. A police car pulled into the driveway. The officer stepped out of his car and said, "I'm patrolling the area and I want you to know I'm watching out for you. If you need anything, just call and I will be here quickly." I appreciated that. As a fellow angler, he knew our son and was concerned for us. He asked how the search was going and if we had any information as to what had happened. Before he left, I asked his name, and he said, "Gary."

The wind was blowing hard at the house. I stared out the window wondering if it was storming at the lake, wondering what was going to happen tomorrow. I did not like that they had to call off the search. That meant more waiting and too much time passing.

When am I going to wake up from this nightmare? What if they never find our son? How will I live with that? How will I live without him? Did somebody do something to him? Was he lying hurt somewhere? Please, somebody! I need answers! God, if he is in the lake, did he suffer? Did he have time to think? Did he struggle? This was too much for my heart to bear. I was confused and didn't understand why this was happening. I had never experienced anything worse than this. *Please, God, this is my only child.* Still, I would have to wait for answers.

Ed said when the town's sirens went off warning of a possible tornado, he prayed that the storm would pass over the search site and not stir the waters. God heard. The storm went in a different direction, and the water remained calm.

Rescue efforts did not resume until 7:30 on Saturday morning. It was cloudy, cool, and windy.

Lord, please help them find our son today.

I stared out into the water. I was tormented by what was going through my mind. It had been three days and nights now. My heart was in agony. I wanted to wake up now. I cried more this day. I was exhausted physically, mentally, and emotionally. Reality began to sink in that we might never find him. All hope of him being alive began to fade. *How are we going to survive?* I could not believe this was happening. I became more distressed, quiet, and withdrawn. I wanted to walk down the path that led under the bridge, where the rescue boats were searching, but was afraid someone would stop me. I felt lost and wanted to be alone. I stayed with the rescue workers more than with family and friends. I watched the divers suit up and prepare to go out in the boats as other divers came in wet and cold. They looked so tired. There was continuous activity around the command post. I remember thinking, *All for my son.* These people were my heroes, and I was truly grateful for all they were doing.

They felt they were close to finding him and narrowing the search area yet again. Our friend, Randy, who is a fire department chaplain, called Ed and asked if he could hold a sunrise service the next day at the lake, for it was Easter. Ed said, "No, instead pray that we will not be here tomorrow. Pray they find our son today." My heart was touched by this request. Knowing our friend, he would pray and ask others to do the same.

Ed and I went to where our friends and family were gathered. He thanked them for their prayers and constant support these three days. He asked one of our ministers to pray the rescuers find Gary today. So the minister prayed with us and our friends and family. As soon as the prayer ended, the chief of police came to update us. As he was explaining what had been going on that afternoon, his phone rang. He said, "They just found him! They're bringing him up now."

I buried my face in my coat and cried. *They're bringing him up? Up from the cold, dark water where he has been three days? God, why didn't You grant my request?* Looking up, there were people all around hugging us and crying. I found Ed's eyes locked on mine. As he walked over and put his arm around me, he said, "Let's go." I felt sick in the pit of my stomach. My mind was tormented by the image of "bringing him up."

It was 3:30 p.m.

We had to tell our parents. I didn't want to do this. They had been pitiful these three days. I wanted to die. *I want to change all this, God! This can't really be happening! Go back three days!*

We hurried down to where they were and declared, "They found him," hoping they understood what that meant. My sisters and nieces came running and we all hugged and cried.

Sometime during all this, our pastor called on my cell phone. He said, "You know that Gary has not been in the water for three days; he's been in heaven." That was something I needed to hear.

How are we going to live without our son? Jesus, help us.

Chapter 2

Extraordinary Champions

During the three-day search, there were fishermen—Gary's friends—searching in their boats with depth finders. They were given permission from the rescue organizations to do this. From one vantage point off a nearby bridge overlooking the lake, I was told that there were boats everywhere. Normal boat traffic had been prohibited in the area. When our son's body was recovered, some of these same boats formed a circle with their vessels. Then their passengers removed their hats and said a prayer. It was a sight I wish I could have seen. I am deeply grateful for them. Jesus has a special place in his heart for fishermen—especially these fishermen.

The rescue workers were so compassionate. They were informative and gentle with us. I still have no idea what all took place there. It was a large operation consisting of thirty-three organizations that aided in the search and recovery.

They kept the media at bay as much as possible and they were careful to give reliable information. The divers we talked to were very cold because the water was only fifty-seven degrees. The water temperature wasn't their only obstacle. Their visibility was only four feet. The only way they had to communicate with those in the boat was a tug on a rope. I have often thought about them and their families. They risked their lives to find our son.

Even the trainers and their cadaver dogs were special. I mentioned the Belgian Malinois, but there was also a Border Collie.

Rescue efforts included running sonar through the nights. There are many more people who did heroic, compassionate work for us. There are many I don't know and many acts I did not witness on those three days. But without these people, we would never have found our son. Even after narrowing the search area down, these people still had to work in an area the size of a football field—an enormous search area in a lake. I am still amazed at their work.

Easter Sunday saw family and friends at our home. For days they packed our home, and brought food and love with them.

I don't know where we would be without our church family. During the three-day search for our son, they made up the majority of the masses of people who came to offer comfort. They prayed for us and with us. They were a constant support and presence. Even though it was Easter Sunday, they came. It is still amazing to me to think how compassionate and loving these people were and still are. We need the body of Christ. We need each other, not just in times of tragedy or crisis but in the good times as well. That is why it is written in Hebrews 10:25 to not give up meeting together, and encouraging each other. Hebrews 13:1 tells us to "keep on loving each other." We need each other as brothers and sisters in Christ. Our church members were not aware that our community witnessed their love and support. I received positive comments regarding them for months to come.

What's more was my own family. My mother, my sister Rhonda and Kristi, kept the house running. They tried to write down the names of everyone who brought food and flowers. They took care of the food and fed everyone. They constantly cleaned dishes, floors, bathrooms, and anywhere they saw a need. Several church members helped with these tasks. For example, my friend, Lydia, asked my mother if there was anything she could do to help. My mother replied, "Can you make mashed potatoes?" My friend told me later that that was the greatest thing she could do, because we needed those potatoes.

My sister Laura took care of everything the funeral home needed, such as pictures, a slide show of Gary's life, and the schedule for the funeral. However she also had help from church members who asked, "What can I do?" She was able to delegate several jobs that needed to be done to help her accomplish this.

Friends and family came and sat with us to give us comfort. Just having their presence was appreciated. Loren would call and ask to spend the night with us wanting to help around the house. She would walk right in and start emptying the dishwasher or some other chore that needed accomplished.

The cards, letters, and food continued to come for months. I had to purchase a trunk to store the cards and letters in, and when it was overflowing and the lid would no longer close I purchased another one.

I intended to read them again after the first year, but, when that time came, I found I just wasn't ready. One day I will be.

Because it was an accident, there had to be an autopsy. They found him on Saturday so the autopsy couldn't take place until Monday. The results from this listed cause of death as drowning. There were no signs of physical damage to his body. Jason, one of the men from the funeral home, was also a fellow fisherman and knew Gary. We called him on Saturday to tell him we would need his services. We went to the funeral home on Easter Sunday to make the arrangements. Even as I write this, it isn't right. Parents should never have to plan their child's funeral. It is not the correct order of things, nor is it something you even think about, or want to. Nevertheless, here we were, forced into this nightmare and the helplessness felt by both of us as parents.

I could not think, and found it hard to make any decisions. Jason was very gentle and patient with us. He made everything proceed smoothly. We had to pick out a casket. When I walked into the room where all the caskets were, I lost it. *Pick out a casket for my son*, I thought. *This isn't right! He should be picking out mine! I can't do this, God!* There was a sickness in the pit of my stomach, helplessness, knowing I had no other choice.

Somehow, with extra strength from God, we managed to do what we had to do. We left there and went to the cemetery to find lots for the three of us. Never did we think we would be purchasing a cemetery lot for our son. I couldn't believe this was happening. We didn't even have burial lots, and now we had to choose one for our son! I wanted a spot at the back near the pine trees. Gary loved the woods and so it had to be near trees. There were three lots together, right near the pines, in the last row.

The next step was to pick out a grave marker. The cemetery director took us in a room and we waited for him to return with a catalog of different options. Before he returned, I looked up and saw a grave marker attached to the wall and said, "That's the one." It had a fishing pole crossed with a hunting rifle and a mountain scene.

All this took less than thirty minutes. God was with us.

We finalized everything and then left.

It was quiet on the way home. Our minds and hearts were full of questions, uncertainty, and disbelief. *What will life be like now? How will we continue to exist?*

Monday arrived and Jason from the funeral home called to say he had received Gary's body. He said, "You aren't going to believe this, but he looks perfectly normal." After all this time, how could that be? God knew we needed to see him one more time. Jason asked if I want him to shave Gary's scruffy beard. "No! Leave him the way he is." I wanted to see my son just as he was.

We had to gather clothes to bury him. We chose his favorite fishing bibs and hooded sweatshirt—the same sweatshirt I slept with a few nights before.

Tuesday came and we could see our son today. I cannot articulate what that did to us. It was something we needed to do, although agony gripped our hearts. Ed and I held tightly to each other as we slowly walked into the room where our son's body lay. I kept my head bowed until I reached the casket. It was the first time we had seen him in six days. I felt the air rush out of me as we approached him. We stood over our son as the tears streamed down our face.

He did look perfectly normal, like he was sleeping. We touched his face, his hair, and his hands. I kept kissing his forehead and wiping my tears from his face. I held his precious hands in mine. I remembered those hands being tiny and holding them for guidance and safety. I touched his turned-up nose that I first noticed in an ultrasound picture and wondered where he got that nose. I know he was a young man, but he would always be our baby, our boy. I could not pull myself away from touching my son, for I knew it would be the last time on this earth.

All this may seem a morbid subject to write about, but death is a part of life and affects all of us eventually. Obviously God was with us, as He is with me now as I relive this to write it down.

Ed and I had the same thought. We chose to have his funeral at church because a funeral home service was just not what we wanted. Our plan was to receive friends on Wednesday from 4:00 p.m. to 7:00 p.m. Except that was not how it turned out. Ed and I had been with family in another part of the church where they had prepared a meal for us. I couldn't eat. What I did try to eat choked me. So we left around 3:30 to see the flowers and be near our son.

When we walked into the sanctuary, we were amazed that it was already filling up. We started receiving friends at that moment. There were so many in attendance that, after two hours, they asked us to move through the crowd, hoping we could reach everyone in line with the time left. We walked from pew to pew and down three aisles. Then we moved out of the sanctuary, down a long hallway to the lobby, out the door, down the sidewalk, around the building, and out to the parking lot, all the while speaking with people. Then we walked across the parking lot to the road before we reached the end of the line.

When we came to the last person, we turned and looked back. No one was around. It was 7:30. An estimated 2,500 people had come. We were amazed! We didn't know everyone. Some were Gary's coworkers, school friends, or fishing buddies, along with his coaches, teachers, principals, and parents of friends. It truly was a tremendous moment.

So many of them struggled with losing their friend. Gary left four grandparents and one great-grandmother. They could not understand why God had not taken them instead.

My parents, who had invested their time and energy in Gary his whole life, and my sisters who treated him like their own, were truly in anguish.

The pastor led the most comforting message that night. Many were encouraged and some even called the church days later to express their gratitude.

I had asked a friend, Chris Seale who is a songwriter and musician, to sing "I Will Rise" by Chris Tomlin. Just a few weeks before, I had asked Chris if he might learn the song and sing it in church. He had sung and played it for me about a week before Gary's accident. Now, as I look back, I know God was preparing us beforehand.

Everywhere I looked, there were pictures of Gary's smiling face, many of them taken the last few weeks of his life. People continually tell me they miss that about Gary. There were testimonies of how he touched other lives and many things he did that we were not aware of. This made us even more proud of him.

The next day, Thursday, was the gravesite service. We met family and friends at the funeral home and they followed us to the cemetery. At the front of the processional were police officers on motorcycles, a friend pulling his boat, the hearse, and Ed and me. Everyone else followed.

We pulled into the cemetery and drove through to the back and over a small hill. Then I saw them! My mouth fell open. I was stunned! I said, "Are all these people here for us?" I had never seen so many people at a gravesite service. The love of all those people just overwhelmed me.

I stepped out of the truck but could not turn my gaze from them. As we walked toward the gravesite, our pastor met us and said, "You won't believe what I found." It was a poem about a child loaned. He asked, "Is it all right if I read it?" I had never heard the poem, but it was something to which I could relate.

Janet Lindsey

A Child Loaned

"I'll lend you for a little time, a child of mine," He said.
"For you to love while he lives, and mourn for when he's dead.

"It may be six or seven years or twenty-two or three.
But will you, till I call him back, take care of him for me?"

"He'll bring his charms to gladden you, and should his stay be brief,
You'll have his lovely memories as solace for your grief."

"I cannot promise he will stay, since all from earth return.
But there are lessons taught down there I want this child to learn."

"I've looked this wide world over in my search for teachers true.
And from the throngs that crowd life's lane, I have selected you."

"Now will you give him all your love, and not think the labor vain?
Nor hate me when I come to call and take him back again?"

I fancied that I heard them say, "Dear Lord, Thy will be done.
For all the joy Thy child shall bring, the risk of grief we'll run."

"We'll shelter him with tenderness, we'll love him while we may.
And for the happiness we know, forever grateful stay."

"But should the angels call for him much sooner than we planned,
We'll brave the bitter grief that comes and try to understand."[1]

Chapter 3

Good-Bye, My Son

When someone we love dies instantly and suddenly, there is no opportunity to say good-bye. It leaves open a door that longs to be closed.

I watched both of my grandmothers die slowly over a period of years—one from Alzheimer's and the other from natural causes.

Seeing them suffer was heartbreaking for our family. As horrible as this was, it gave us the opportunity to say our farewells.

I feel blessed in that I did not have to watch my son suffer and die from a terminal illness. My heart aches for those who have to endure those circumstances. My son died while he was full of life, doing what he loved to do.

It wasn't until after the funeral and the commotion of activity in our home slowed down that I had an overpowering need to talk to Gary. There were questions I wanted to ask and things I wanted to tell him. Not questions regarding his accident, or words I wished I had said and never did, but just an everyday conversation while enjoying his presence. I needed to see him physically and touch his human body. I needed to say good-bye.

I've read accounts of ceremonies or family rituals that gave grieving people a specific way to say good-bye to their loved ones. Others were able to hold their deceased loved ones for one last time. This brought the closure they so needed.

Ed was one of the last people to see and talk to Gary as he left for the lake that day. The last words Gary said to his dad were, "See you later, Dad."

Writing this book has helped me deal with my grief just as writing the below poem allowed me to say good-bye to my precious son. There is great comfort in knowing that my good-bye is not final. I will *see my son later.*

Good-Bye, My Son

I keep waiting …
      For you to call home.
I keep watching …
      To see you come through the door.
I keep listening …
      To hear your voice.
But time goes by,
      The phone doesn't ring,
And I see …
      The door remains closed
Though I hear,
      The sound is silence.

I did not get to say good-bye
Before you left and went away.
Now I am here asking why.
Oh, to have just one more day.

It is so hard to let you go,
My child, my very own.
Tearing my heart apart to know
You're gone, and it feels so alone.

The separation seems much to bear,
As endless days and nights pass by.
I have shed many a tear,
And have even wanted to die.

I know in heaven, where you are,
God has for you a divine mission.
Even though you seem very far,
You see it all with clear vision.

I'll be there one day before long.
Be waiting when I appear.
We'll be together where we belong,
And there will be no more tears.

For now, and only for a while,
   Good-bye, my son ...[1]

Chapter 4

Letter to Gary's Friends

During one of my sleepless nights, I lay in bed feeling sorry for my son because he had no idea that he was going to die that day.

At twenty-two, you don't think about dying. You have your whole life ahead of you. One of our conversations the day he died was what he was going to do when he came home. He had plans.

As I lay there and thought of this, I wondered what Gary's friends were going through, having lost one their own age. Had they felt invincible? Had they ever thought about death? Did Gary's death leave them questioning their immortality? If I could talk to his friends, what would I say to them? What would God want me to say to them?

At that moment, the words started flowing so fast that I had to jump out of bed and write them down. The tears were flowing as I wept through the whole letter. I could not see the screen for the tears; I hoped my hands were on the correct keys. When I finished, I went back to bed. When morning came, I reread the letter, realizing there were important truths throughout. Having a relationship with Jesus is there. Hope is there. God's sovereignty is there.

Since I believe God gave me those words to write, I prayed over the letter before I mailed it to many of his friends, hoping someone's life might be changed.

June 23, 2009

To Gary's Friends,

The past two months for Ed and me are hard to put into words. Our grieving hearts ache for our son. If we could have one more day, give one more hug, scratch his back, hear his big laugh … but we can't. We long to see his truck pull in the driveway while country music is beating on the radio and see him smiling. We sit in the garage some days like we are waiting for that to happen, except it doesn't. The phone rings and we wish it were him, but it won't be and will never be again. The reality of this is at times overwhelming. We feel we can't breathe, we can't get out of bed, we can't go on. Life goes on, but we feel like the world should stop because the person we love the most is missing.

Gary's life was a short twenty-two years, but it was full. If I didn't believe the verse in Psalm 139 ("All the days ordained for me were written in your book before one of them came to be."[1]), I would be struggling even more. But I do believe our days are written in the councils of heaven, and there is nothing we or anyone else can do about it. If I didn't believe my son was in heaven and have the hope that God promises us, I couldn't go on. I would be curled up in a hole somewhere and dying for lack of hope.

When Gary got up that morning he was full of life. We had breakfast together just like most mornings. He was looking forward to the upcoming tournament as he hooked up his boat. He had an exciting day breaking in a new boat, being on the lake all day. He made twenty-eight calls that day from his phone. He called me five times talking and laughing. He was full of life.

I tell you this because Gary never knew he was going to die that day. He had plans. Plans not just for the day and week but for life. He wanted to get married one day and have kids. He had plans. He never knew. I can't say that enough. Most of us don't get out of bed every morning and think this could be our last day. No, we live thinking we will be old when we die. But we aren't promised that. We don't know. And for this reality, I write this letter.

I've heard Ed tell people old and young, "Don't let your family stand over your casket and not know where you are. Have your life right with the Lord so they'll know without a doubt where you are." He's right. Gary made that decision when he was nine years old. He told me, just recently, that at some point he doubted that he was saved so one night in his bedroom he made *It* right. I found a small Bible in his room this week that let me know when that was because he wrote it down. That doesn't mean we are perfect and never make mistakes; we are human. It means we know when we've done wrong we confess and repent of those wrongs. I saw in the last three weeks of Gary's life changes he was making. Things he knew he needed to make right. Conversations we had, songs I heard him singing, and other ways confirmed this.

The bottom line is this: If you don't know Jesus, now is a good time. You may not have tomorrow or the rest of the day—you don't know. If Gary could speak to you, I know he would tell you the same thing but in a much stronger sense. He is experiencing a life we can't even comprehend. And if he had the opportunity to come back, he wouldn't. He is more alive today than he ever was.

> The door of death is merciless in its finality. You cannot snatch even one precious second to say the thing you wish you had said or do the thing you wish you had done. You cannot reassess your values then, nor change the course of those events that careless unconcern of worldly attitude allowed to rise. When God calls your loved one Home, He simply takes him in and closes the door, and that is that. Weep as you will, love as you cannot help but love, long as your being longs, there is not one word that you can say, one thing that you can do to make anything different. Today if you hear His voice do not harden your hearts.[2]

Thank you for being a part of Gary's life. His life was rich with friends, and we will hold on to all the great memories.

Janet

Chapter 5

Carry Me

I do not feel sufficient in giving advice on how to cope with grief, since I still deal with the process every day. I don't have myself *together*.

It encouraged me to be able to relate to someone else's grief and realize I was not alone in my struggles. Through my journey in sorrow, I have poured myself out in order that it might help others, and in doing so I have found strength.

The experience of grief is different for everyone. No one truly knows us like God, and He alone can offer the understanding we search after. I have considered my times alone with God as sacred; I have poured out the depths of my soul. Each one of us coping with grief, I believe, can relate to this: It is our grief, our suffering. This may be why we experience new and different emotions after loss. Anger can rise quickly when we feel someone is interfering with *our* grief. We feel he or she is unaware of the anguish with which we endure so therefore we put up a shield to protect us. On the other hand, compassion has established a home in our hearts like never before.

My hope is that my journey will offer someone else hope. The only real hope we have in this world is Jesus. He promises life everlasting. He suffered, died, and was resurrected to give us that hope. I pray that as I share my daily struggles, you may be encouraged to know you are not alone and be able to see that God is with you to comfort and strengthen you. He will carry you when you are weak. When we stumble under the pressure, He is there to help us back up. He alone can grant the peace of mind and heart that passes all understanding.

Early in this grief journey, I felt helpless and devastated. Still in shock and disbelief, there were times when my mind wouldn't rest and I could find no peace. I wanted immediate relief. I was tired of crying and tired of the torture. Despair was setting in at this point.

Crying out to God helped me verbalize my troubled thoughts. I knew my help would come from Him, but He did not work on my timeline. At this stage, it was hard to understand why God would allow such afflictions to crush me. I wanted to talk to Jesus about some of His promises and ask Him to fulfill those in and through me at that very moment, in my great time of anguish.

> He gathers the lambs in his arms and carries them close to his heart.
>
> Isaiah 40:11

> I have made you and I will carry you.
>
> Isaiah 46:4

> God, You have ripped my heart to pieces! I feel alone. Where are You God? I'm dying inside. This emptiness is devastating. I want to run from it,

avoid it, but it chases me down. The air is being sucked out of me. I am drained of strength and energy. There is a battle going on within me fighting despair and panic.

I think I'm going to lose myself.

My son is not coming back. I am stuck here, not moving, and I don't have a choice. Everything has changed. From this day forward, life will never be the same. Why didn't I die before him? He had his whole life ahead of him. He would have made it much better without me than I am doing without him. My passion for life has vanished. The desires of this world have diminished because what I love the most is in the next world.

Jesus,

Your Word says we can come to you when we are weary. We can come to you when we feel we can't go on. It seems everything is crashing down around me. I've been cast into complete darkness. I am hurting and heartbroken, Lord. Bring the comfort that only You can give.

I know that nothing catches You off guard, but I have been thrown off my feet. I know You determine my steps, but I cannot get up. Please carry me.

Chapter 6

This Isn't Fair

Why do the wicked live on, growing old and increasing
in power? They see their children established around
them, their offspring before their eyes.

Job 21:7–8

Life is not fair. I don't understand God's ways, but He doesn't
have to be fair. Life did not treat Jesus fair. He was rebuked and
rejected, ridiculed and spat upon. The people, in their wrath, nailed
Him on a cross to suffer and die.

One day shortly after Gary's funeral, I was in the yard feeding
the birds. My two dogs were running around and playing. I stood
and watched the birds and the dogs and thought, *This isn't fair! Why
do my dogs and these birds get to live?* That they were still here and not
my son made no sense.

On days I would have to go into town, I would feel a heaviness
all over me. I felt like I was seeing the world through a fog. Watching
the cars and people going in many directions, I would think, *Who*

are all these people? Why can't my son be one of them? Why do they get to live? Why can't I just die?

I believe Job thought about unfairness. Why else would he ask God why the wicked grew old and enjoyed wealth and power? They even had the pleasure of being with their children and grandchildren, while Job, a righteous man, lost all his children, his wealth, and his influence. Asaph asked the same question of God in Psalm 73.

Somehow we want to think that if we go through life doing everything we know is right and true, we are protected from pain and suffering. However, when life's storms arise, the strong faith to which we profess is tested. We aren't exempt from trouble. I found myself asking the same question as Job. Why does wickedness live on and good die? Why do some lives never acknowledge that there is a God and prosper while godly people experience suffering?

Jesus said, "In this world you will have trouble."[1] He knew we would experience struggles and disappointments. He knew that today I would need Him more than I ever have.

After Jesus said we would have trouble, He said, "Take heart."[2] Have hope. I know I can pour out this soul-wrenching sorrow to Him.

Job's conclusion has to be mine. When God finally spoke to him, all he could do was stand in awe. He never received an explanation for his suffering or answers to his questions, though his godliness was proved. Job knew God was God and that He could be trusted even when it did not seem fair. Asaph realized that God was always with him, holding him by the hand, guiding him with His counsel, and in the end would take him into glory.

My whys seem never ending, never finalized. Yet I sense God is not going to answer these whys. He doesn't have to explain whether He is fair. He is just and right in everything He does. In my heart and from His Word, I know God makes no mistakes. He, for some reason, allowed this tragedy in my life. No heartache can touch me without first going through Him.

Chapter 7

Suffering and Sorrow

Sorrow runs deep and leaves scars. Sorrow and loss should drive us to God and cause us to reexamine our lives and seek out the Lord. God says, "You will seek me and find me when you seek me with all your heart."[1] My sorrow and loss will be with me the rest of my days. I will always be aware that my son's life was cut short. All the dreams we had for him, and his future, ended suddenly, leaving us alone without him. Life has forever changed. Every day I wake up with this immediate thought: *My son is gone. Another day without him. Another day to deal with the grief and empty house without his presence. Another day of tears.* Job said, "Surely, O God, you have worn me out; you have devastated my entire household!"[2] "Days of suffering grip me."[3] "When I looked for light, then came darkness. The churning inside me never stops; days of suffering confront me."[4] Oh for the days when my child was around me.

> Suffering has no meaning unless we can believe that
> God understands our pain and will comfort us.[5]

I don't know why I have been tested with such a tragedy, but I do know this: God can grant His immeasurable grace and strength through all difficulties and sorrows, leaving us aware of how needy and dependent we are on Him. He lovingly holds me in His arms and comforts me. Like Job, I know I can cry out to God.

> But I have found comfort knowing that the sovereign God, who is in control of everything, is the same God who has experienced the pain I live with every day. No matter how deep the pit into which I descend, I keep finding God there. He is not aloof from my suffering but draws near to me when I suffer. He is vulnerable to pain, quick to shed tears, and acquainted with grief. God is a suffering Sovereign who feels the sorrow of the world.[6]

I have asked God, "Why did You allow this when You had the power to let Gary live?" I have had a difficult time with that question, struggling to comprehend how all this works out in His perfect love. Since we don't have any answers to what caused the accident or how it happened, and it all seems a mystery, why are we left not knowing, disturbed by these thoughts? Why my son?

I have been angry with God for allowing this, and I have yelled at God. I struggled with praying for a time. All my prayers ended up at the same place: drenched in my sorrow and loss. I know God is attentive to my heartache and confusion and understands more than anyone.

Someone has said that asking why is a faithless question. I say it's not true! And some people say asking why is not trusting God to be God. But if I did not ask why, I would question my humanness. I would be more like a robot with no feeling. Must I be so formal with God that I can't speak from my heart? Can I revere Him *and* feel welcomed to pour out my soul? Asking why, from the depth of my heart, is evidence that my relationship is that of a child to her heavenly Father who knows all her thoughts anyway. What I have learned is that my Savior can handle my whys, my anger, and my frustrations.

When Sorrow Comes

When Sorrow comes, as come it must,
In God a man must place his trust.
There is no power in mortal speech
The anguish of his soul to reach
No voice, however sweet and low,
Can comfort him or ease the blow.

He cannot from his fellow men
Take strength that will sustain him then.
With all that kindly hands will do,
And all that love may offer, too,
He must believe throughout the test
That God has willed it for the best.

We who would be his friends are dumb;
Words from our lips but feebly come;
We feel, as we extend our hands,
That one Power only understands
And truly knows the reason why
So beautiful a soul must die.

We realize how helpless then
Are all the gifts of mortal men.
No words which we have power to say
Can take the sting of grief away –
That power which marks the sparrow's fall
Must comfort and sustain us all.

When sorrow comes, as come it must,
In God, a man must place his trust.
With all the wealth which he may own,
He cannot meet the test alone,
And only he may stand serene
Who has a faith on which to lean.[9]

Chapter 8

Contemplations from Job

What I feared has come upon me; what I dreaded
has happened to me.

Job 3:25

The blessings of my child in the past remind me of what I can't
have for the future. Everything I went through wanting a child,
and then the joys of raising him, now reveal the depth of my loss. I
knew God's Providence had blessed us with this boy. I could envision
a wonderful future for him. At twenty-two, he was past *raising* and
had developed into a fine, young man. I felt proud to tell people he was
my son. When his life was taken from him, I was shocked that God
would permit that to happen. My anger was directed to Him, because
I knew, that in His Sovereignty, He could have prevented it.

The day I wrote the below journal entry, I was outlining my life
to God: *I prayed for a child, You gave a child, then You take him back?*
I was angry and confused. I wanted an explanation.

All I wanted was a child. After enduring health problems, surgery, and more health problems, it did happen. This little creation was my child, my baby. When the day finally arrived, I heard his soft cry—like a little lamb. I immediately wanted to hold my baby! But they rushed him away and I had to wait to see him. In my heart I kept saying, *Please hurry, I want my baby!* Finally, they placed him in my arms and yes, God, I heard You speak in my heart, "He's my child." I very clearly heard You, and I had a choice to make. I knew what to do. I decided this: "He is Your child, God. Thank You for him." I prayed every day for that baby, little boy, teenager, young man, and every day You reminded me that he was Yours.

In my heart, I knew he was special and that You had unique plans for his life. I could not wait to see what You were going to do through him. Then *You took him away from me!* My thoughts changed. *What about those special plans? God, I prayed for him every day! I don't understand! Wait! Don't let this happen!* I couldn't be there for him when he really needed me! I felt like Job when he said,

Why have you made me your target?[1]

If he snatches away, who can stop him? Who can say to him, what are you doing?[2]

It made no sense! He is my only child! I felt so helpless and wanted to blame God. I was paralyzed with no motivation. I wanted to hide from the world. I thought, *Will I endure the rest of life just going through the motions? How will I cope from now until I die?*

There have been times when I felt so angry, I wanted to stomp my feet and scream, just like a child having a tantrum and demanding her way. I wanted to change it all. I thought, *I don't like this!* No, no, no! But, I knew I had no choice and no control over the situation.

Again, the words of Job made that clear.

> But he stands alone, and who can oppose him? He does whatever he pleases.[3]
>
> I know that you can do all things; no plan of yours can be thwarted.[4]

Then, one morning during time with God, He came close and let me know this was for me. He said,

> "Have you ever realized whatever concerns you concerns Me too?" He kept speaking through His word, "For whoever touches you touches the apple of my eye" (Zechariah 2:8). "You are precious and honored in my sight" (Isaiah 43:4). "Are you experiencing a time of sorrow?" "This is my doing." I am "a man of sorrows, and familiar with suffering" (Isaiah 53:3). I have allowed your earthly comforters to fail you, so that by turning to Me you may receive "eternal encouragement and good hope" (2 Thessalonians 2:16).[5]

The deeper my love, the deeper my grief. My grief is immense because the love for my son is beyond measure. God pours out his infinite grace on me even more.

> Devoted Father,
>   I take great encouragement and hope from the fact that my son belonged to You. That I am

reminded of that so often is a truth I dwell on for solace. You are a compassionate and gracious God. Even in my anger and disbelief, You have shown me Your love and have drawn closer when my heart has cried out to You.

The LORD gave, and the LORD hath taken away; blessed be the name of the LORD.

Job 1:21 KJV

The Sunday before Gary's accident, he was out of town until late afternoon. I missed him that day more than usual and was waiting for him to come home. When he arrived, I gave him a big hug and told him how much I missed him. We played a board game with his friend all evening, enjoying every minute.

After his accident, the realization that I would never be able to hug him gripped my heart. It did not matter how much I missed him, there wasn't anything I could do about it. The hurt from missing him is sometimes more than I can bear.

Writing letters to my son somehow helps me deal with my grief.

I Miss You

My heart is so heavy, my son. I miss you so much. I am so sorry I was not there to help you when you needed me most. I miss your presence and your voice. ***I would have died for you.***

I miss your laugh, our talks, and scratching your back. I even miss your messy room. Everything about you I miss. I wish I had cooked more for you and hugged you more often. I'm so sorry for all the days I seemed too busy. I can't believe you're gone. I have no more passion for life. I get out of bed every day only because God has given me the grace to. I think of you continuously.

I have to work, and your dad needs me, so I have to go on. I'm not contributing much to this world right now. I can't imagine living another twenty years without you. That is beyond what I want to think about. I need to talk to you. I want to sit and just enjoy being with you. The ache in my heart is great knowing I can't.

I wasn't through being your mom; I didn't have enough time with you. I am so proud of you. I always was, and I am so glad that your dad and I told you that often. You were a pleasure to raise. You were unusually mild tempered and easy to get along with.

I keep thinking about that last Sunday we were in church together. We were sitting next to each other. The choir started singing their special and you whispered, "I like this song." Then you started quietly singing, and I saw you saying the words, "The Lord gives, the Lord takes away, blessed be the name of the Lord." Now I wonder about that. The Lord reminded me of that very early on.

I wish I could remember everything we talked about that last day. The last call you made on your cell phone was to *home*. You just didn't know that in few minutes you would be at your final home. Now home is where you are, son. It sure isn't here. I want to be where you are and be with you. I will be there one day soon. I wait for that day with great anticipation.

Chapter 9

Who Are You, God?

God's Providence can cause struggles in our mind. When I wrote this, I was beginning to experience God in a different way. As a result of Gary's death, I found difficulty in identifying with this part of God's character.

> God, I had lived my life to know You more. I've prayed not just to receive what I asked, but to know You more. To know Who You are and what Your purposes are.
>
> I thought I knew You.
>
> Where were You that night when I begged for my son to be alive? Where were You for three days while they searched for him? Why would You allow us to live three days not knowing if our son would ever be found? Why did we have to endure the thought of him under cold, dark waters? This part

of You, God, I don't know. I have never experienced You like this.

You have been to me a God who blesses. The God who helped me through trials and temptations. I had not experienced the God who allows horrible tragedies to happen to His very own. Yet why did I think I was exempt.

Mark records the last journey of Jesus and his disciples into Jerusalem: "They were on their way up to Jerusalem, with Jesus leading the way, and the disciples were astonished, while those who followed were afraid."[1]

Referring to this verse, Oswald Chambers, a gifted, insightful teacher of the twentieth century, said the following:

> At the beginning we were sure we knew all about Jesus Christ, it was a delight to sell all and to fling ourselves out in a hardihood of love; but now we are not quite so sure. Jesus is on in front and He looks strange.
>
> At first I was confident that I understood Him, but now I am not so sure. He is ahead of me. I have no idea where He is going, and the goal has become strangely far off.[2]

I know Jesus is with me, comforts me, and gives me grace and strength, but I no longer understand Him. Perhaps I never did. I'm not sure where He is leading me through this. This wasn't what I had in mind. This wasn't the future I saw. There is a mist that I can't see through. A strange fog where there are no explanations, no answers from Him, and only questions from me. There are times when I don't feel God, but I know He is here. He says in His Word that He is. So whether I feel Him or not, whether I understand Him or not, I know He is with me. His plans will succeed with or without my understanding. All I can do is follow His lead.

Chapter 10

When God Lifts the Hedge

God knows our pain and can be trusted even when it goes beyond our capacity to understand. What significance could come from the loss of a healthy, energetic, fine, young man in the prime of his life? I didn't have the answer to that question early in my grief. As time went on, I began to see ways God was working in the loss. Trusting God meant I was living in the hope His Word speaks about and relying on Him to open my eyes to see Him working. If I could accept this sorrow, and offer it to God, maybe He could use it for His purposes.

The Bible says Job was righteous and good. He honored God in every way. He covered his family in prayer and God blessed Job in every way. God had a hedge of protection around him and everything he owned.

We pray for our children and our families. We pray that God will bless us, protect us, and put a hedge around us so Satan will not be allowed to intervene and harm us in any way. However God allows Satan to send us momentary trials and light afflictions throughout our lives to test us and to strengthen our walk with Him. Sometimes we allow those trials and afflictions to consume us and, instead of running to God with our needs, we depend on ourselves to get through. We sometimes fall into the trap of believing that if we are doing everything we know to do as a Christian and stay in fellowship with the Lord, then He will continue to always have that hedge of protection around our family and we will always be safe and fine.

God has blessed our family through the years. He had kept us safe and granted the protection I requested. Then one day, the worst happens and I wondered, *Where was God*? The hedge seemed to have disappeared.

Job loved and cared for his children. He was their spiritual leader and pursued that call by offering sacrifices for their sins. He guided them in the ways of God. Satan told God that he could not get to Job, because God had a hedge around him and everything he owned.

And God lifted the hedge.

But why, why would God allow Job, that righteous man, to suffer as he did? Job never understood. He came to know God in a way he had never known before, but the question is still there.

When God lifts His hedge, we experience deep wells of grief and sorrow that run so deep that our former trials and afflictions are almost insignificant. When God lifts His hedge, we see Who is in control. When God lifts His hedge, our lives forever change. When God lifts His hedge, we have to acknowledge that our God allows inexplicable pain. When God lifts His hedge, He is all we have.

Job is one of the greatest examples of trusting in God in the Bible. In the battle between God and Satan, God won. Job never saw the battle being fought; he only lived it and came to a greater faith. I feel confident that one of the reasons we have the account of Job's life is so people like me, who have experienced loss and a lifting of the hedge, can relate.

Chapter 11

The Cemetery

For those of us coping with grief, there are rituals we can carry out that may help us endure. These rituals can somehow have a connection to our departed loved one, something that was of interest to him or her. Meeting at the gravesite and having a time of reminiscing about our loved one, where butterflies or balloons are set free to soar to the heavens, can be a comfort for some. Candle-lighting ceremonies can be held to honor the memory of loved ones.

Since I love the outdoors and gardening, Ed and I created Gary's Garden from over one hundred flowers, plants, and trees we received at Gary's funeral. The garden is quite large and requires year-round upkeep, but this is something that helps me cope. It is therapy for my soul.

Going to the cemetery on a regular basis is not for everyone but it is something I need to do, and I usually go alone. It is not something Ed wants or feels the need for. I have had unexpected experiences while visiting there.

One day I pulled to a stoplight when a hearse pulled beside me. My mind was flooded with thoughts of following one with my son's body inside to the cemetery. It was the last time I would be near his body in this life. I love his body; it is part of my own. The thought created an ache in my chest, and I began to weep.

Some may wonder why I go to the cemetery every few days. Here's why: I know Gary is with the Lord and not in that grave, but his body is there; I love his body. This ache in my chest, this longing for my son, will never leave. It will be with me the rest of my life. The *what could have been* will always be there. I trim the grass and bring flowers, keeping them neatly arranged. I do all this just so I can do something for him.

Separation anxiety compels me to visit the cemetery. That yearning to be near him.

Close to my son's grave, there are other young men in their twenties. One day the mother of one of those boys was there while I was. No words were exchanged between us. She was only twenty feet away. We just stood by our sons' graves. I thought, *Oh God, did that sight hurt Your heart? I know You feel our pain.* "You've kept track of my every toss and turn through the sleepless nights, each tear entered in your ledger, each ache written in your book."[1]

About a month after Gary's accident, I was in the cemetery on a beautiful clear day. I stood over his grave and looked up into the sky. There was one cloud, and it was directly in front of me. The cloud was in the shape of a fish, a perfect brim. I watched until it broke up and left a cloudless sky. I knew that had been for me.

On one day, while I was trimming the grass around his headstone, I had this uncontrollable need to dig and dig until I could reach him. Frustration flared up from helplessness and an all-consuming need to hold my son: I just needed to touch him. This separation was more than I could bear! I beat the ground furiously with the trimmers. I had to leave; I couldn't contain my tears as I gasped for air. I felt heaviness all over me.

Recently when I was there, my mind was anxious from work and the cares of the world. When I arrived, I heard a baby bird trying to chirp, but all that came out was a high-pitch screech. I went about trimming as usual, but the bird kept on. I looked around once to see if I might spot him. When I did not, I kept working, lost in my thoughts. The bird seemed to screech more loudly and more constantly. I thought, *Maybe God is trying to get my attention.*

I put down the trimmers and stood up, looking around the ground for the little fellow. He wasn't on the ground but in the pine tree that was right next to me. There in a nest, sitting out on a limb, was the little bird, his head bobbing up and down. His sound was so piercing and constant that I said out loud, "I hear you and I see you!" Suddenly he became completely quiet. I could still see his head bobbing around, but he never made another sound. He had my attention. I then looked around to make sure no one heard me talking to a bird.

I decided to take a picture of him in his nest, so I ran to the car and got my camera. While I was taking the picture, a truck pulled in and stopped. A young woman got out, walked down to a nearby grave and started organizing the toys and flowers that had been placed there. It was a new grave and the articles around it had lured me over one day to see that he was an eighteen-month-old boy.

I heard the young woman sniffle and knew I had to go over and speak to her. She was the mother of the child. I told her I was sorry for her loss and that my son was here. She said she knew my son, had gone to middle and high school with him, and visited his grave occasionally. We talked a few minutes about how hard it was dealing with our losses. I noticed on the grave marker her son was born in October and died in April, same as my Gary.

There were moments of silence that had me keenly aware of the stillness standing there in the cemetery. The wind was blowing, the bird was quiet, and God was there with us. When I left, I told her I would pray that God would comfort her.

The day we followed Gary's hearse to the cemetery, I was still in shock and waiting to wake up from the nightmare. My heart had been shattered. My life felt as if it had ended and there was no tomorrow. I thought, *there goes our only child whom we poured our life into for twenty-two years.* His future was more important than ours, his needs ahead of ours. He was our joy.

Chapter 12

Grief Journey

You cannot run from grief. It is always there. You can run from your problems, bury your burdens, and ignore your responsibilities, but grief ... it will attack at any unknown moment. It demands to be addressed every day.

Shortly after the accident, I was in the grocery store when a grief attacked occurred. In every aisle there was a food item my son liked, and I regularly purchased, staring me in the face. I found myself reaching for an item and then drawing my hand back. *I don't need this anymore, ever again.* It was like shoving a knife in my chest. Grief gripped my heart and uncontrollable tears would start to flow. I wanted to scream from the pain and run away to hide.

I don't know how, but I finished shopping that day. There wasn't a way to plan around the attacks because they were random. They had to be dealt with independently, in the loneliness of my heart.

The loss of our son faces us constantly. Grief is something we never *get over*. Either we let it take us down the road to despair and depression, feeling as if there is no hope, or we come to a place where we have to accept the loss and accept the fact that we can't change what happened. We cannot go back. So we learn anew every morning that grief must be dealt with again, today, moment by moment.

I have traveled down the road to despair and depression, where darkness and emptiness dwell. Down that road, there is a lack of motivation and concentration. For a while, everything seems meaningless. Why should I take care of myself anymore? What's the point? The end is still the same: my son is gone, and that fact if irreversible. More than once I've traveled that sad, dark road.

At some place, I found I had to turn around and come back. I am a believer in Jesus, our only hope. I can't dwell in the land of *no hope* for long because I have put my hope in the living God, "Who is the Savior of all men, and especially of those who believe."[1] He has promised us hope, and He keeps His promises. Sometimes God provides health care professionals to help us when we have no strength or desire to come back, and that is okay. When I was in my early twenties, I suffered from severe depression over circumstances in my life. All I wanted to do was sleep so I would not have to think or deal with life. My doctor recognized this before I did and was able to help with medication. I thank God for that doctor.

Hope is a word I have come to cherish. A word I depend on. Hebrews 10:23 says, "Let us hold unswervingly to the hope we profess, for he who promised is faithful." I desire to be loyal to my Only Hope.

Jesus *will* return and join us with our believing loved ones, who have already died. I rest in this promised hope.

Ed and I have learned about grief. We had grieved the loss of our grandparents several years earlier. We had grieved over sin and opportunities in life that failed. However, this grief was new to us.

At first, it was very confusing. There were so many emotions running through our hearts and minds. Realizing we had to deal with this was exhausting. Some days we wanted to give up and die, not work at analyzing the new and dreadful feelings.

We grieve completely different from one another. Ed is outgoing and social. He loves to be around people. Part of the way he grieves is to talk about his feelings with his friends, especially those who want to talk about our son. He is also energetic. Keeping busy physically helps his mind stay focused on other things. He cannot sit and dwell on our loss or he will become depressed. Ed has many friends who are always asking him to do things. He would go fishing or help someone work, anything to occupy himself. He always asked if I cared, knowing he would be gone for a while. I understood he was dealing with his grief in this way and never protested.

I keep most of my thoughts to myself. On extremely troubling days, I obviously write them down instead of talking about them. I can look at pictures of my baby and watch DVDs of his life while crying all day, but I prefer to be alone while doing so. I read other people's stories of their grief to be able to relate. All my emotions and anguish are dealt with as they come, many times over, and each one is evaluated.

We have learned to allow each other to grieve in our own way without criticizing. This has been essential for our relationship.

At church we have a dear friend, Bob, who was with one of the rescue groups. He was actually on the boat when they found Gary and brought him up.

One Sunday he came to give us a hug, and he asked, "Are you two okay? Are you drawing closer to each other?" I'm sure I gave him a strange look the first time he asked me that. No one had mentioned this to me up to this time. The second time he asked, he explained how the death of a child could either draw a couple closer or tear them apart. I appreciated his concern and gave this much thought. I began reading of instances of this and learned the divorce rate is high among couples who have lost a child.

Ed and I were close before our son's death, but this has drawn us closer. Everything hasn't been perfect. For weeks I was troubled over the night he called me at church to tell me of the accident. One day I lashed out at him and asked, "Why did you call me only one time? Why didn't you just keep calling? Then I would have known something was wrong! By the time I got to the lake, word had been spread and other people knew before I did! I'm his mother!" He explained that he was driving over one hundred miles an hour and the rescue squad was calling and asking questions about the boat, and he just didn't have a chance. In my heart, his answer was not good enough for me.

On other occasion, we decided to get away for a weekend and go to one of our favorite little towns in North Carolina. It was a hard decision to make. Part of us wanted to go, but we also felt the need to stay home. We were both depressing to be around. We started arguing about whether we should take this trip. The tension kept building, knowing we were about to drive over the bridge where they had found our son.

We cried as we went over it and remained quiet for a while. But when we came to the North Carolina line, we started arguing again. Before turning around and going back home, we pulled off at a walkway that led into the woods. We walked and cried for a while and then made the decision to take the trip.

We were so glad we did. We needed it more than we ever realized. I feel that was a vital choice we made in our relationship that day.

We are the only ones who truly identify with each other. We have accepted our differences in dealing with our loss.

Through our grief, we have learned we need each other. More importantly, we need God. We may plan our day, but, by God's Providence, those plans could change instantly. God sits on His throne and engineers our circumstances. He is sovereign over the universe, over creation, and every detail of our lives. He has been with us every moment through this journey and will never leave us or forsake us.

At the beginning of this grief journey, I questioned His Providence. Although I believed my faith was strong before this happened, my faith was tested. Ironically faith is my spiritual gift. There were questions I had to answer for myself.

Chapter 13

Tested Faith

When Jesus teaching became too hard for some of His followers, many of them turned and no longer followed Him. Jesus asked the twelve, "Do you also want to leave?" Peter replied, "Master, to whom would we go? You have the words of real life, eternal life. We've already committed ourselves, confident that you are the Holy One of God."

John 6:66–67, The Message

Lord, I have thought so much about where all this takes my faith. Have You let me down? Is there some promise that wasn't for me? Where else would I go for help and strength?

These questions were asked many times over. I remember the day I considered giving it all up. Why even try? I was doing my best and this is what happens? I wondered if my faith up to this point made any difference to God, or was He so far out in space that He didn't notice? That day was a turning point in my walk with the Lord. I sincerely searched for answers to those questions, which brought on more questions. Was God trustworthy? Were His promises valid? Could I still serve a God who had allowed such tragedy in my life and follow Him even though I didn't know where He was leading? I wrestled with these questions and feelings that God didn't even care, He wasn't even listening. Why would He not answer my suffering soul and justify Himself? If I chose to live without Him, what would be the consequences?

As frightening as all this had been, life without a sovereign God was a fearsome thought. I had to choose which path I would follow. I desperately wanted to believe in God, for somehow a purpose would exist. Without Him, there really was no purpose for life or anything.

I was so sure of the direction I thought He was taking me, and I was thrown off my feet. I thought my dependence on God was settled before Gary's accident, however, when I was faced with what seemed like a senseless tragedy, it became a real test of faith.

> During times of severe testing, even the best theology can fail you if it isn't accompanied by experiential knowledge of Me.[1]

I realized I could not predict God's ways. I am dependant on His every lead. There is nowhere to go and no one else to turn to. You have the words of life. You have our life. I am not in control. I am helpless without You, Lord. You have all the answers that I long to hear. You have my very life in your hand. "My times are in your hands."[2]

Oswald Chambers puts it this way:

> Faith never knows where it is being led, but it loves and knows the One Who is leading. The life of faith

is not a life of mounting up with wings, but a life of walking and not fainting.[3]

Not knowing where I was being led in this journey of tested faith caused more struggles to try to understand. I had to fight my way to a place where I could let God be God, and trust Him.

Recalling one of those nights when I was plagued with trusting God, I wrote in my journal attempting to answer the questions of faith.

> What strength do I have, that I should still hope?
> What prospects, that I should be patient?
> Do I have the strength of stone?
> Is my flesh bronze?
>
> Job 6:11–12

> What happened to my son? All he wanted to do was go fishing! Sometimes the need to know is overwhelming. This conversation with God was mostly one sided. I was doing most of the talking. However, I pictured Him intently listening to me as if I were the only one on earth. As my mind settled down, I heard, "Trust Me." I know He loves me. He hears me. He gathers my tears. He feels my pain. Even though He doesn't answer my questions, I still have the need to ask them. "Trust Me" has never been more of a test. In my heart, I know I can. I know His word and His promises and they stand forever, whether I see them being fulfilled or not.

I didn't feel His grace even though He had covered me with endless amounts. How else could I have possibly lived through this? I'm not dying for lack of hope. I get out of bed every day by the strength granted to me. How else could I have functioned? This grief has been consuming. It has been exhausting. There have been so many emotions I'd never experienced before. Anger has never been an issue with me, but grief brings anger to the surface. I found myself angry at God, angry at comments that were thoughtless, and angry at myself for being angry!

On the other side of this emotional roller coaster, I had a tremendous amount of compassion for others going through grief. My mind was a constant whirlwind of struggling activity. On days like that, I felt weak and began to second-guess myself. I asked questions like *What if I had done this or that?* I wondered if that would have changed anything. Generating regrets only led to despair, and feeling sorry for Ed, Gary, and myself. I knew I could not handle this alone. I realized that faith and belief in God were my only options. There simply were no other options. I needed God.

When Job was tested, Satan said he would fall. However God knew otherwise. Some days I honestly feel like I am in a spiritual battle. Satan thought I would lose the faith. He has heard me in the past ask God to increase my faith. He has heard me say to God, "You are my life, my breath, and an all-consuming fire." In the front of my Bible, I have written that God is the very reason that I am. I have my life's verse there: "My flesh and my heart may fail, but God is the strength of my heart and my portion forever." [4]

Faith in God that is tested through a hell-on-earth, and stands, is true faith.

Several times, I wrote in my journal of the struggles with faith and coping with my loss. On many sleepless nights, scenes of Gary's accident tortured me. Scenes I never witnessed but imagined. This was one of those times.

> God, I can't bear it today. All night long I woke
> and reality came crashing in again. "He's gone?"
> I couldn't believe it. Yet he wasn't here, anywhere.
> His presence, his voice was absent. My need to talk
> to him and not being able to was more than I could

stand. It was tormenting to want someone so much but there was absolutely nothing I could do.

My questions continued: What about the lifetime of prayers for my child? Every day I prayed for You to protect him, to draw him to You, God. I prayed that he would hate sin, be responsible, respect people in authority, choose the right friends, choose the right mate, submit to You and resist Satan, and be a young man after Your own heart. *What about those prayers?* A few months before his accident, I prayed that he would love You, God, with all his heart, soul, strength, and mind, that he would desire Your ways.

While he was growing up, we took him to church weekly and taught Him that You were the whole purpose in life. I remember when we was just three years old, he would say, "Momma, Jesus is Lord!" He couldn't say r's, so it was especially cute, but he had already learned a profound truth! We understood it was our responsibility to teach godly, moral values to our son, and we did this the best we could.

You said, God, that if we ask anything according to Your will we have what we ask for.[5] I know You hear my prayers. Were you telling me that the fulfillments of my prayers were being accomplished in heaven?

God, I have more questions. Did Your angels come and protect him from struggling in the water? Give me comfort from the torturing thoughts of my son in the water trying to survive, and from wondering what he went through, and what he might have been thinking. Was he scared or were

You right there with him? Did you need him for some assignment in heaven? What is he doing?

I know everything You do is out of love for us. And Your purposes and plans no one can alter. Nevertheless I am struggling, again, tonight, with these thoughts.

Peace from this seemed to take forever. It made me think of people who had actually witnessed a loved one die in an accident. How locked in their minds that scene must be that they cannot get free from.

I have a close friend, Kathy, who was at our house many times during the days after the accident. She told me that Gary had not suffered. I asked her, "How do you know?" There was a peace she experienced that God took him before he struggled. Knowing this woman, and her walk with the Lord, this statement encouraged me and brought me comfort.

Another friend came by one day to tell me she had a dream of Gary, in the water, with a peaceful look on his face.

It was two years before I would sleep soundly through the night.

I still have days, or nights, when my vivid imagination is like a recording I want to shut off. I would like to encourage someone going through this process, as a lady at our church encouraged me. God can use our terrible, sleepless nights to test and strengthen our trust in Him. He is the Prince of Peace and that peace will eventually come. It may be something we have to continue to ask for from time to time, as I do, but He alone has the peace that passes all understanding, and that is the kind of peace we need. God grants us peace as we trust in Him. It is not always easy, while enduring tragedy or loss, and it does take an effort of will. God is worth the effort.

Faith grows during storms. Remember when you see a person of great spiritual stature, the road you must travel to walk with him is not one where the sun always shines and wildflowers always bloom. Instead, the way is a steep, rocky, and narrow path, where the winds of hell will try to knock you off your feet, and where sharp rocks will cut you and prickly thorns will scratch your face, and poisonous snakes will slither and hiss all around you. The path of faith is one of sorrow and joy, suffering and healing comfort, tears and smiles, trials and victories, conflicts and triumphs, and also hardship, dangers, beatings, persecutions, misunderstanding, trouble, and distress. YET, "In all these things we are more than conquerors through him who loved us (Romans 8:37)."[6]

Janet Lindsey

Be Still, My Soul

Be still, my soul: the Lord is on thy side.
Bear patiently the cross of grief or pain.
Leave to thy God to order and provide;
In every change, He faithful will remain.
Be still my soul: Thy best, thy heavenly Friend
Through thorny ways leads to a joyful end.

Be still, my soul: thy God doth undertake
To guide the future, as He has the past.
Thy hope, thy confidence let nothing shake;
All now mysterious shall be bright at last.
Be still, my Soul: the waves and winds still know
His voice Who ruled them while He dwelt below.

Be still, my soul: when dearest friends depart,
And all is darkened in the vale of tears,
Then shalt thou better know His love, His heart,
Who comes to soothe thy sorrow and thy fears.
Be still, my soul: thy Jesus can repay
From His own fullness all He takes away.

Be still, my soul: the hour is hastening on
When we shall be forever with the Lord,
When disappointment, grief, and fear are gone,
Sorrow forgot, love's purest joys restored.
Be still, my soul: when change and tears are past,
All safe and blessed we shall meet at last.

Be still, my soul: begin the song of praise
On earth, believing, to Thy Lord on high;
Acknowledge Him in all thy words and ways,
So shall He view thee with a well pleased eye.
Be still, my soul: the Sun of life divine
Through passing clouds shall but more brightly shine.[7]

Chapter 14

A Different Way

I'm living a different life. Everything has changed. My old life was better by far. I'm not saying God hasn't given us blessings since Gary's death; He definitely has. Along with grace and strength, He has showered us with love from family and friends. He has given us new friends. People have been so kind and generous to us, so we are blessed with many friends. Some blessings can only come through adversity: blessings of proper perspective, priorities, and realizing life's purpose in a more devoted sense. He has always blessed us by meeting our needs. However the loss we feel is immense.

I remember after they found Gary, and we came home, I went outside to walk around the yard. Everything looked different. The trees were not the same. The flowers and grass all were changed. This stirred strange feelings in me. My backyard seemed odd, surreal, like I was walking in a dream. I find myself looking up into the sky so often now, looking for signs in the clouds, believing God speaks in His creation.

My life has changed. The things I did in my other life don't have the same appeal. Holidays lack the excitement they once had. It's hard when we are all together, because Gary is missing. Somewhere I have read that after a tragedy and loss you have to find a *new normal* for your life. I do not like that term because *nothing* is normal. I hesitate to find a new way because some days I would rather die and go home. On the other hand, I know what they are saying. Life is not the same, and I can't go back to the way it was. I cannot change what happened. So, in my struggles of living from day to day, I'm discovering this different way. As much as I want to reject finding a new way, I *must* find it.

Just now, as I'm writing this, a bird flew into my window. It was a baby wren all fluffed with feathers and trying to fly. I startled him when I stood up to watch him. He called furiously for his momma. Quickly she came and showed him the way to go, and they flew off together. When I sat back down, I picked up my devotional and read for this day.

> As you listened to birds calling to one another, hear also My Love-call to you. I speak to you continually: through sights, sounds, thoughts, impressions, Scripture. There is no limit to the variety of ways I can communicate with you. Your part is to be attentive to My messages, in whatever form they come. When you set out to find Me in a day, you discover that the world is vibrantly alive with My presence. You can find Me not only in beauty and birdcalls, but also in tragedy and faces filled with grief. I can take the deepest sorrow and weave it into a pattern for good.[1]

Since this tragedy, life has changed. I have changed. I have been more aware of God speaking in different ways and want to keep my eyes open to see God work in this sorrow. He knows how to speak to us. And He will, if we will keep our ears open to hear, our eyes open to see, and our hearts open to understand.

God knows how much I love birds, so it seems only fitting that He uses birds to communicate to me. When the baby wren lost his mother, I felt like God was saying, "As Gary's mom, you took care of him, led him in the right path in life, and now you have to let go and let him fly so he can be all I intended for him to be."

In God's Providence, it is designed for some to die young. Gary had an ordained day, just as you and I have. Now God would take my sorrow and loss and "weave it into a pattern for good."

Chapter 15

Happy Birthday, Son

We felt powerless when our son's birthday arrived six months after the accident. I had always enjoyed baking a cake or pie and buying him gifts. But there were no gifts, no cakes; we didn't even have him.

I needed to tell my son how proud I was of him and his life and that he lived it well. This helped me survive the day. It was extremely meaningful for his friends to post comments on Facebook. Their reminiscing and kind words truly blessed my heart. Receiving cards in the mail was also a kind act.

October 27, 2009

Happy birthday, my son.
It has been a rainy, dreary day.
I miss you. I miss cooking for you a birthday meal.
I wanted to buy you something. Earlier today, your
dad and I went to your favorite store. We just needed

to get out of the house. We saw all kinds of things we wanted to purchase for you.

Do you realize how many people love you? Your Facebook memorial page was bombarded today with people saying how much they love you, how much they miss you and that big beautiful smile. You had more friends than I ever realized. You touched so many people's lives. It just amazes me. I wish I had been more aware of this when you were here.

The day you were born, your dad, who was nervous about having a baby, carried you around the hospital like a football. He was so comfortable holding you. You cried like a little lamb. You were a good baby, a good child. Most people can't say this, but you were even a good teenager. You never gave us any trouble. You were a fine, young man, and I am so proud of you.

It is very comforting to read what everyone wrote about you and to you. Makes me even more proud. I just wish I could tell you, again, today on your birthday.

I love you with all my heart,
Mom

Chapter 16

Jesus Goes Before

They were on their way up to Jerusalem, with Jesus
leading the way.

Mark 10:32

He calls his own sheep by name and leads them out.
When He has brought out all his own, he goes on
ahead of them, and his sheep follow him because
they know his voice.

John 10:3b-4

When grief comes in like a flood and we feel we can't go on, it helps to picture the Savior of the world leading us to places of rest. We feel like we've lost our way and need the guidance of His strong hand. Let Jesus choose our path, and follow His lead.

Jesus goes before us, always leading the way. He knows what is around the bend before we do. He sees what we do not see. He understands how everything works together for His glory. Sometimes

He leads us to pleasant places. Sometimes He leads us down paths we don't want to go, down paths we would never ask to take. He is always with us, leading us.

I never dreamed we would go through this. Yet, we are here. This is our story and we have no choice but to be in it. I keep thinking about Jesus going before. Since He knows what is ahead, He knows how to take care of us when we reach that place. Just like a shepherd caring for his helpless sheep. Yes, even through the valley of the shadow of death, He is with me.

> Your Shepherd is with you at all times. You never have to call Him into your situation. You never have to wonder where He is. You never have to fear that if things become too difficult, He will abandon you. He goes before you; He walks beside you; He comes behind you. He protects you securely. Just as He sees every sparrow and knows every hair that is on your head, so His gaze is constantly upon you. He comforts you with His strong presence in times of sorrow and grief. He leads you through the valley of the shadow of death. He does not necessarily lead you around the valley as you might wish. There are times when your Shepherd knows that the only way to get you where He wants to take you is to lead you down the path that passes through the dark valley. Yet, at those times He walks closely with you, reassuring you throughout the journey that He still loves you and is with you.[1]

Our Shepherd always does what is best for His sheep, just like good parents always do what is best for their children. As parents, we are continuously concerned for their welfare. We think about their needs, even when they become adults. We never stop being parents or caring for our children. Then one day, we are led down that valley of death, and it is our child. All of a sudden, we are not required to meet their needs or be concerned for their life. All that is gone in an instant. How do we stop this process, this devotion we've had for years? I found myself picking up the phone to call Gary or thinking of something I wanted to ask him when he came home.

What path am I being led down now? I'm not always sure, but as long as Jesus, my Shepherd, is leading the way, I can rest in His loving arms, knowing He cares infinitely for His sheep.

Chapter 17

Fishing in Heaven

Is your night one of bereavement? Focusing on God often causes Him to draw near to your grieving heart, bringing you the assurance that He needs the one who has died. And as this thought enters your mind, along with the knowledge that your loved one is engaged in a great heavenly mission, a song begins in your heart.[1]

It comforts me to think of Gary in heaven. I can see him with his gramps and papaw. Both of these great grandfathers were fishermen and hunters. I imagine them sitting beside a beautiful, crystal-blue lake in the green plush grass on the outer edge of a deep forest. The sky is blue with big fluffy clouds. They hold fishing rods as they relax and reminisce.

I imagine that deer walk out of the forest, and they admire the animals as they catch big bass and release them back into the lake. They are laughing. They are content. The apostle Peter comes with his rod and sits with them too. Peter tells them what lure to use to catch the big ones. After all, he has been there longer and knows the lake better. Gary is so happy. The great grandfathers are finally enjoying their great grandson. They didn't have much opportunity on earth to do that.

Finally Jesus comes and joins the group. They fall on their knees to worship Him. Then He shows them how to do some serious fishing.

I said, "I imagine," but I realize this could very well be the scene in the present heaven. Jesus told the thief on the cross, "Today you will be with me in paradise."[2]

Fishing with Jesus could be Gary's paradise right now.

I also image Gary on a heavenly mission. Gary's name means "mighty warrior." When he was small, he would dress up like an Indian complete with war paint, or he would wear his Davy Crockett outfit and coonskin cap. I always reminded him what his name meant.

A mighty warrior on a heavenly mission is also a comforting thought. I imagine that Gary knows the purpose behind everything that happened to him. So now he is on a mission designed by God—fulfilling that purpose.

Imagination is a gift from God. He wants us to use this gift for His purposes. We have all imagined what heaven might be like. I use my imagination in this way to bring peace and comfort to my soul. It brings a longing for our real home, where we will be together with our Lord.

Chapter 18

"How Are You?"

It had been six months and it seemed the grief was getting worse. I desperately *needed* to do something for my son. I left his dirty clothes in his basket for two months before I could wash them. I just wanted things the way they were. But I also wanted to do something for Gary. On one particular day, this motherly need was overpowering. With anguish, I washed his clothes, smelling each article as I placed them in the machine. After drying them, I gently folded them, placing them back in the basket. I knew that would be the last time I would ever perform that task. Then, after three months, I thought I would die if I couldn't do something for him. In his room I spent two hours dusting, vacuuming, and straightening up. I didn't remove the sheets or bedspread. That would take his smell away. I didn't move anything out of its place. The need to be his mother is strong, and the emptiness consumes me.

I believed that no one could comprehend what I was going through. Many people, including me, are in a habit of saying, "How are you?" It is a standard greeting. I never dreamed that that simple question could cause such emotional turmoil, because it was a question without an answer. I couldn't say, "Fine," because I wasn't. I could say, "Do you really want to know?" But I really didn't want to tell them. So I found that if I just asked them right back "How are you?" without ever answering their "How are you?" I got away with it. At some point, I started saying "Okay," but that was not the truth. It simply became a way to satisfy the person who was asking without having to search for the right words—words that had escaped me to this point. Some actually replied, "Really? I'm so glad to hear that." Inside, I would scream, *Are you kidding? Do you really think that I'm okay?* For a while, I found it easier to avoid people as best as I could, all so that I could avoid that question. One person actually asked Ed, "Are you over it?" That came only two months after Gary's accident, and it was the worst question either of us has ever been asked. The answer, of course, was, "No, we will never be over it."

This caused me to wonder if I had ever asked such a question of someone who was hurting from a loss. After this experience, I realized that the best thing to do is to not ask a question at all. What was meaningful was knowing that friends were there when I needed them. After all, what is there to say?

Some of my friends would hug me or take hold of my hand and give it a squeeze without ever saying a word. That meant much more than words. Others said, "I'm still praying for you." Those words were kind and encouraging. But, "How are you?" was not comforting. Even if the question could be answered, I thought, *How long do you have for the answer? How deep into the depths of sadness and loss do you want to plunge with me to really know how I am?*

Some suggested I should go back to my way of life before the accident. My way of life will never be the same. *I* will never be the same. Tragedies and loss change you forever.

These comments and questions, though they may have been inappropriate, came from friends who genuinely love us. It was apparent they had no idea of the profound grief we were experiencing.

They were unaware of the intensity of this kind of sorrow. I am grateful for them and their concern for us. Their prayers are cherished.

I have a close friend, Tracy, who is very busy with a full-time job, a husband, and a family. She is active at our church too. Right after the accident, she made a point to come by every week to have coffee with me. She never seemed rushed but sat with me and talked. I'll have to say, I rarely opened up with her. Maybe only two or three times did I even try. I just found it too difficult. So we would chat and have coffee. I knew if I ever needed to cry, talk, or break down, I could with her. She has been a constant support and treasured friend. After two and a half years, she is still coming for coffee.

I have other friends who have sent cards every month or so.

These acts of love are significant for helping with the loneliness accompanied with grief. Just to know someone is thinking of me helps to ease my pain.

It can be difficult to know how to help someone who is grieving. At times the bereaved are so distraught they are unable to make suggestions. Ed and I were this way. It is important for the church and friends to show compassion to the grieving. Advice is usually not wanted. Telling us "time heals" will not go over well either. It was obvious when we were avoided, as if we had the plague, but to acknowledge us is to show you care, even if you don't know what to say.

What is needed is practical help and friendship. Our church, family, and friends amazed us with their thoughtful, imaginative support. They would call with a suggestion and ask if it was okay to proceed with the idea. There were so many deeds of kindness, and I wanted to share some of them.

Two men from church, who know Ed always has clean vehicles, called one day to say they were coming over to wash our car. Another friend and his son knew we had cut a dead pine tree and it was still lying in the yard. They sawed and chopped until we had a nice stack of firewood. When we were preparing to make the memory garden, friends brought equipment and tilled the garden spot. One man from church, who had lost his young son to cancer, called and begged to do anything. He knew the importance of helping the grief stricken. A dear couple who own a restaurant called many times and asked us to come for supper. They would sit us in a private corner and feed us well. My hairdresser came to my house and styled my hair. A friend stopped by to give a manicure. Another friend, who owns a paint store, stained our deck. Another has a landscaping business and had our yard mowed for weeks. Ed's cousins and their wives invited us to eat or go places with them many times. A friend had an artist create a portrait from one of Gary's pictures.

The ideas these caring people had seemed never ending. We have been blessed with people who offered their services, time, prayers, hugs, and a tremendous amount of love. God placed them in our lives to encourage us. I cannot mention all the generous acts of concern, but they are remembered with a truly grateful heart.

Chapter 19

Identity Crisis

Loss thus leads to a confusion of identity. What is left to enjoy after having lost so much that was so dear?[1]

Jerry Sittser

People have said, "Time will heal." Time will *never* heal my loss, but time may change how I view the loss. Life will never be as it was before. Sorrow lasts a lifetime. Some things we will never get over, but we must go on. Life hasn't stopped for us. It isn't waiting for us to pick ourselves up. It goes on, with or without us.

The day after Gary's funeral, Ed had scheduled surgery for a torn rotator cuff. That was the last place we wanted to be that day, but we had no choice. He was in tremendous pain and it had to be done. We had to work, even when there was no concentration. Our friends and family had their lives and their families. It was hard just trying to have a normal conversation.

How I respond to what has happened will determine how I go on. Will I live in despair and depression the rest of my life? Though I have those days, I know I can't stay there long. God cannot be glorified in lives that are bitter and despairing. I understand how someone would want to live a life of isolation, avoiding the challenges of answering to people who do not understand. However that isn't the response God wants from me.

Going through this has given me empathy and understanding for others who are suffering. Recently a woman from my church passed away and left a husband and two teenage daughters. I looked across the church one Sunday morning and saw the oldest daughter. She was crying and the look on her face was one of distraught. My chest started to ache—for her and for me. What was it like to lose a mother? Our circumstances were different, but they were both of loss. The mother in me wanted so much to hold her and comfort her. If I had died before my son, I would have wanted someone to reach out to my grieving child and comfort him.

I walked across the church to hug her and tell her I was praying for her. As I hugged her, I could feel her pain. I felt my pain. I no longer had a living child to mother. My identity for twenty-two years had been *mom*. Now I am a childless mother.

We gave ourselves to our son and we joyfully devoted our time and energy to his life only to have to let him go. We will never hear the words *mom* and *dad* from our child again. Not in this lifetime. How do I go on each day and live without the joys of my son? What is my identity now?

When I hear children calling, "Momma," I want to take hold of that mother and say, "Do you hear that? It is such a sweet sound! Your children are precious and you are privileged."

Chapter 20

Death Is a Teacher

D eath is a teacher.
Death teaches that you're not in control.

It is a helpless feeling unless I am trusting in God. Sometimes it is frustrating because I want the controls. I want to figure out the whys and hows, yet the Lord has not given me any answers to these questions. I become discouraged only to haul myself up and believe in God's promises. From kindergarten until the time Gary could drive, I drove him to and from school. Every afternoon when I picked him up, I would ask, "What did you have for lunch today?" "How did you do on that math test?" "Who did you play with on the playground?" I wanted to know what he had been doing when I wasn't with him, and I liked knowing the details. As he got older, I could tell he wasn't as enthused about me asking ten questions every afternoon. One day, bless his heart, he said, "Mom, please, no more questions. I'm tired."

So when the answers to the most important questions I have ever asked God seemed to go unanswered, it is disheartening. God promises; He is Sovereign over the universe. He has said that our days are ordained. There is an appointed time for us to be born and to die. He is saying He has our lives in His hands. We have to come to the place of destitution, where we realize we can do nothing, and we are powerless and insufficient to help ourselves.

Then we can let God be God and trust that He has everything under His control.

Death teaches God's ways are not our ways.

God is so big. He sees and knows the whole portrait of life down through the ages. He works things out according to His will and His purposes; not mine. As I have commented before, I saw my future, my son's future, different from how it has turned out. I could picture him married and with children. Those grandchildren I was going to love and enjoy will never be. I don't understand God's ways. If I did, I would be like Him. I need God to be my everything. As my Creator, He knows me better than I know myself, and He knows what is best to fulfill His purposes.

Death teaches this is not our home.

There is more than this life. Jesus has gone home to prepare a place for me so we can all be together, forever. That is my real home. I look forward to going there now more than ever. Heaven is the goal, the final reward. I desire to finish this race well and go home.

Death teaches trust.

Trust God even when circumstances are beyond understanding. This is not as easy as it sounds. I want answers. Why does God allow children to die before their parents? Why does God allow mass destruction through acts of nature? Why does God allow the horrors we face in this world today? I want faith that sees, which is really no faith at all. I want to see the reason for it all. However, faith that cannot see a thing but believes and trusts is pleasing to God.

Death teaches priorities and perspective.

Some things are petty and small. Leave them that way. Death puts a bad day in perspective. Know what truly is important in life:

God, family, friends, helping others, and serving the Lord. Love those who are still here and tell them how much they mean to me.

Death teaches compassion.

When we've gone through the shadow of death, we have more compassion for others who are going through the same. We can comfort those in their need, as we have been comforted. I have had the heartbreaking opportunity to show compassion to two women who lost their sons after I lost Gary. When we meet someone whose pain is similar to ours, we connect and speak the same language. We can openly cry with each other and feel each other's pain. Since I am a few months ahead of them in my grief, maybe I can help with thoughts and struggles they are experiencing.

Death teaches dependency on God.

I need God. I recognize that He is the One who can calm the restless, sleepless nights. One can find this rest in God whenever a decision is made to seek Him out for our need. When we decide *Yes, I want and need God,* we don't just sit back and wait. We have to do something. We have to put forth the effort to read His Word on a daily basis, searching the Scriptures for peace and comfort. We have to be willing to be honest with God and pour out our hearts to Him in prayer. He is the One who soothes the soul's intense agony of separation and loss.

Chapter 21

Compassion to Empathy

When I saw the movie *The Passion of The Christ*, I had a different perspective on Jesus's death. I was horrified that He went through the torture and pain for me. It was my sins, even petty ones, which caused His death. I was ashamed and yet intensely grateful of His love for me. Galatians 2:20 tells me He "loved me and gave himself for me." That is personal.

Something else agonized my heart in that movie. I watched as Mary witnessed her son being tortured and beaten, spit on, ridiculed, and then nailed to a cross as she watched Him die. He went through that for her too. I remember my chest aching for her as compassion filled my heart. I thought, *I could never bear losing my son.* How did she go through that? He was always there, always with her, and had even prepared her. The only way she could have endured the anguish of losing her son was by His grace. I just had never thought about that part of it before.

That memory came back to me one night as I lay in bed and thought of my son. Yes, I thought I could never bear losing my child and yet the grace of God has been right there. There have been times when I thought I could bear it no more and I was going to fall apart at any moment. But at just the right time, He comes and brings the grace I need. I can't explain grace. I just know God has poured it out on me. We know grace is undeserved favor. It is a gift from God. He gives grace to everyone. If you are breathing, God gave you the breath.

I have asked for grace. About a year before Gary's accident, I learned a new way to pray from our pastor. He said, "Ask God for grace so that you can be all that He wants you to be. Ask God for guidance so that His hand would be upon you. Ask God for growth so that you might serve Him in a larger capacity. And ask God for godliness so that His hand of protection would be upon you until you finish this race, and pray you finish well." I believe I received grace, because not only did I ask for grace but also God is generous and has an abundant amount to give.

Chapter 22

One Year

We received many letters from friends telling us how Gary's life and death had influenced them. We treasured these letters and read them many times. On the one-year anniversary of his death, I wrote Gary a letter. I had become depressed during this time. Actually, it started creeping in over the winter. I was on the verge of tears continually. It took months to get through the shock and disbelief, and now reality had made its home in my soul: my son was gone and was not coming back.

> My son,
>   You have been gone one year. I miss you so much. My heart aches for you.
>   It seems like only a few days. Where has the time gone? I want the time to go by fast. The sooner I will see you again, the better my soul will be.

The winter was cold, dark, and long. We have grieved desperately for you. I study your face in your pictures. Every feature I know so well. Your room still smells like you. I think that is a gift from God.

The season is changing and spring is in the air. Spring is a time of new life, but it will always remind me of your death. Easter will always be bittersweet. Our Savior rose and gave us eternal life, but your life ended right before Easter. Because Jesus lives, you live, my son.

In this past year, we have seen and heard of all the lives you touched when you were here. If I touch half as many people as you, I will have accomplished much. I always knew you were special.

How have I made it without you? Only God knows. When I come to heaven, I will see just how much He did help me.

I know you are completely happy and that is a comfort, but it doesn't take the endless days and nights of pain away.

I cannot wait to see you again. I will be there soon. Be waiting for me.

I love you forever,
Mom

Chapter 23

God Is Able

There have been days of discouragement when I honestly wanted to give up, just give up praying and talking to God, seeking Him for my needs. I didn't want to make it through another day. I was tired and worn out. I was unorganized and had no enthusiasm with life or anything else. It seemed like I took one step forward and three steps back, so why should I even try? I would revisit areas I tried to work through, like the *what if's*, only to realize they needed more work. I needed peace from these areas but there was no relief. I lacked the motivation to do anything constructive.

The first thing I do every morning is go to God and His Word. I have been doing this for so long I couldn't stop if I wanted to. The desire to know God is so strong that I must spend time with Him. On the days of complete despair, I realize how much I need Him. God is the only place to go when I feel like giving up.

I have found that God has time for me. He listens to me and hears all my questions and complaints. He is an encourager. He draws near to those who have broken hearts. If we ask God to speak to our hearts through His Word, and honestly seek Him, He will give us verses of Scripture that will be just for us at just the right time. He knows what we need before we ask. His ways are sometimes hidden from us, and His dealings can seem unkind. Faith must work its way into my soul where I know God can be trusted. He is the God who sees. He is my stronghold and He remains steadfastly true.

What would my life say if I gave up from weariness? What would that tell all the faithful believing friends and family who have prayed continuously for us? Would it tell them that everything is meaningless? No, like Solomon, when we come to the end of our questions, to the end of our self, we will say, "Fear God. Do what He tells you."[1] He will bring everything to light one day and my questions will have answers. My grief will end and my tears will be gone forever.

Until then, God is *able*. He is "Able to do immeasurably more than all we ask or imagine."[2] My creator, Who knows me better than I know myself is *able* to meet every need I could possibly ever have. He is *able* to keep me from falling. [3] So on the days I feel like giving up, He is there, picking me back up. Notes from a friend or an encouraging call are some ways God uses His people that have helped push me forward. A verse of Scripture speaking directly to me is another way. I am strengthened whenever someone tells me how Gary's life made a difference to them. Jesus prays for me too. When I don't know what to say or I am too downhearted to speak, He lives to intercede for me and He is "Able to save completely those who come to God through him."[4] He asks, "Do you believe that I am able to do this?"[5] Yes, Lord. When I feel like all the plans and dreams and prayers are nothing but a mist, I remember these words: "He is able to guard what I have entrusted to him for that day."[6] There is comfort in knowing that nothing "will be able to separate us from the love of God that is in Christ Jesus our Lord."[7] Not even death.

There are so many ways God comforts and encourages me. I love to walk with my dogs in the quietness of the woods. God loves us so much that He cares even about the small things, like giving us pets. I thank God for my dogs. Besides being fun to watch, they make me laugh and this comforts me. For a while, they occupy my mind and let it rest.

Chapter 24

A Great Fisherman

Gary had been fishing in the Heartland Angler Tournaments. In this fishing series, the anglers have to fish at least four tournaments in their division and qualify for the classic held at season's end. Whoever is leading at that time is recognized at the annual banquet and wins the grand prize. Gary and Jacob were near the top of the leader board when his accident occurred. Their 2009 annual banquet was held at Guntersville Lake in Alabama. The president of the Heartland Anglers at that time was Bill Burton. He invited Jacob, Ed, and me to attend. They honored our son and gave us a plaque dedicated to his memory. When they presented the plaque, everyone stood and applauded. This meant so much to us and truly touched our hearts.

Here is what the plaque says.

Dedicated to the memory of a great fisherman and friend.
May your smiles always be remembered and your memories
Forever kept in our hearts.

Chapter 25

The God Things

A few weeks after Gary's accident, our songwriter and musician friend, Chris, came by with his wife, Ramona. They are precious friends who have prayed continually for us. I was with them the night I got the call of Gary's accident. After I left church that night, Ramona gathered church friends to pray for us.

We talked about the "God things" we experienced since Gary's accident. We walked down to Gary's garden to show them the lovely flowers. They brought us a beautiful blanket that had an imprinted image of a father and son fishing. They also brought a CD with Gary's image etched on the front. Chris had written and recorded a song about Gary titled "I Am Your Father, You Are My Son."[1] He told us the desire to write this song was weighing heavily on him. He could not rest until it was completed. We didn't listen to the song until after they left that night.

The song talks about father and son walking side by side through autumn's grassy fields. A few months after he wrote this song, we took down a trail cam that Gary had used for hunting. The camera had taken a picture sometime in the fall of the last year Gary and Ed had gone hunting together. They were walking in autumn's grassy fields, side by side. We called our friend as soon as we saw the picture to let him know. Another line in the song says, "See you later, Dad." Those were the last words Gary said to his dad as he was leaving for the lake that day.

This was a most memorable work of love, a true gift to us.

I Am Your Father, You Are My Son
A Tribute to Gary Scott Lindsey
©Christopher Seale

I was there; when they placed you in your mother's arms
A gift from heaven; we vowed to keep you from all harm
And I had visions; of the man you would become
I am your father … you are my son
I was there; the day you spoke your first words
You said Daddy; at least that's what I heard
And I'm the one; who taught you to walk before you run
I am your father … you are my son

Forever part of this family conceived in love
A blessed union that's ordained by the Father up above
He has given us a lifeline that reaches to the distant shore
Tell me how, could this family ask for more

I was there; when you cast your first fishin' line
And when you caught one, I took a picture in my mind
Oh you were smiling, as if you caught the only one
I am your father … you are my son

Side by side we walked through autumn's grassy fields
All the beauty, and God's presence was so real
And like creation, you realized where you came from
I am your father … you are my son

Forever part of this family conceived in love
A blessed union that's ordained by the Father up above
He has given us a lifeline that reaches to the distant shore
Tell me how, could this family ask for more

I was there when you said yes Lord I believe
One simple prayer; and I heard angels start to sing
He is the anchor: no matter where the winds blow from
He is our Father and you are His son
I was there when you traded your cap for a crown
And when your spirit flew, we placed your body in the ground
"See you later, Dad," I guess my work on earth is done
He is our Father, we are His sons

Forever part of this family conceived in love
A blessed union that's ordained by the Father up above
He has given us a lifeline that reaches to the distant shore
Tell me how, could this family ask for more

A few days after the funeral, Gary's best friend, some of his buddies, and relatives were looking to purchase a GPS. They wanted one identical to the one Gary had on his boat. While they were in the store, they turned the screen on to the one they were interested in and the cursor appeared on the spot in the lake where they found Gary.

One of Gary's good friend and fellow fisherman, Doug Pressley, decided to plan a memorial fishing tournament to honor Gary. So on July 3 he held an all-night tournament and called it The First Annual Gary Lindsey Memorial Firecracker Fishing Tournament. It was only three months after the accident and I really didn't know how hard they all worked until the day of the tournament. When I saw the fishermen who came to support the tournament, I just couldn't believe my eyes. One hundred and thirty-one boats rolled down the ramp and sat in the cove at the Fort Loudoun/Tellico canal, waiting for the blastoff. As they took off, I felt the tears running down my face. It touched my heart to see so many people support this. Gary would have loved this event.

Doug was so well organized and the tournament ran smoothly. Most of the proceeds went to search-and-rescue organizations that aided us during our time of need.

The Second Annual Gary Lindsey Memorial Firecracker Fishing Tournament saw 157 boats fish and raised $4,000 to help a fire—and-rescue organization. Before the boats blasted off at 7:00 p.m., the announcer prayed that God might grant a window from heaven so Gary could see his tournament. There had been a large cloud cover hiding the sun earlier that afternoon. As soon as he prayed that prayer, the sun's rays beamed through portholes in the clouds. Everyone who saw this took pictures and commented. My friend, Erin, presented me with a framed picture of this. The verse from Hebrews 12:1 was printed on the picture: "Therefore, since we are surrounded by such a great cloud of witnesses, let us throw off everything that hinders and the sin that so easily entangles, and let us run with perseverance the race marked out for us."

The Third Annual Gary Lindsey Memorial Firecracker Fishing Tournament raised $9,200 for the two chapters of the American Red Cross, and had 167 fishing boats. Awesome!

I have a friend, Angie, who works for the Red Cross. We met years earlier when she was Gary's swimming instructor. Angie later married a friend of Ed's, and we reconnected then.

During the three days at the lake, Angie searched the banks with other Red Cross volunteers and friends. She walked and looked until she was exhausted. She remembers, "I needed to find him. He has to be here because *he can swim!*"

She recalls being very upset for not finding anything, when she heard in her heart, "Stop! Stop looking. Gary's not here. He is with Me." Distraught, she sat down at the place where the boat had come to rest and saw something shining in the water. Angie then clearly remembers hearing in her heart, "Take this to his momma." She picked up a rock in the shape of a bird, and it even had an eye. Knowing how much I loved birds, she was overwhelmed with emotion. She knew this was a sign from God.

Several weeks later, she came by to bring me the rock. She told me the story and then gave the "bird rock" to me. I was amazed.

I handed the rock to Ed. He turned it over and announced, "It's a fish, with an eye."

Angie had not recognized this and we all sat there stunned.

This rock is my comforting sign from God.

When people come to visit, I love telling them this story and showing them the rock. The reaction is always the same: "I've got chills!" They rub their arms, take a closer look, and shake their heads. It is truly a miracle.

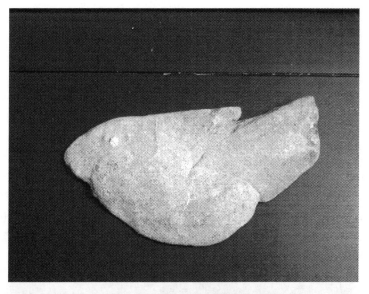

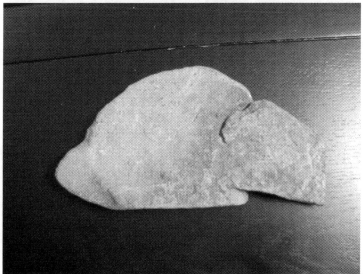

Many friends and family gave us outdoor plants to honor Gary. With the help of a landscaper friend, Sam Love, we used the plants to make our beautiful memorial garden that continues to thrive and grow. Since then, we have been given all kinds of garden accessories, including a bird bath, bird house that chickadees nested in the first year, a little bear with a fishing pole, a fish, garden rocks, a sign that says, "Gary's Garden," an arbor, chimes, benches, shrubs, flowers, and trees. One of the benches was made from cedar and the back is engraved with some of the words from a book about loving forever. The bench was special because it was made by the men over the rescue operation.

I have had a secret mailbox friend for a year. On many occasions I checked for mail only to be surprised by a little bird ornament, a fish, or a gift. A sweet note, sometimes with a verse of Scripture, almost always accompanied the gifts. But the notes were never signed. I still do not know who the thoughtful person(s) is. Nevertheless, this was a thoughtful way to show their love.

Several months had passed when Gary's cousin, Ott DeFoe who fishes professionally, was in Okeechobee, Florida. He had just finished fishing a tournament and was heading home.

He and his wife pulled into a fast-food restaurant when a small truck pulled beside them. Its driver rolled down his window and wanted to talk to Ott. The stranger in the truck asked Ott if he would buy him something to eat. Ott walked inside with the man, and they started a conversation. While they were standing in line to order, Ott asked the man if he was a Christian, and the man said that he was. The man began to quote Scripture. One verse in particular stuck with him: "Never will I leave you, never will I forsake you" (Hebrews 13:5). Ott thought it was strange that he would quote that verse. After they received their meal and were parting ways, Ott asked for the man's name. He said, "Gary."

Ed has a Volkswagen that he restored. One day he was looking underneath it, as he had hundreds of times while working on it. This time he saw something hanging from a wire. As Ed took a closer look, he saw that it was a fishing lure, a rooster tail, just hanging there perfectly. Neither the hook nor the lure was bent. It was another simple but comforting reminder of Gary and God's grace.

When they found Gary, his keys, ChapStick, wallet, and cell phone were still in his pockets. I found it incredible that, after three days in the water, these items were still in his pockets. I took his cell phone to the store where he purchased it to see if there was any way we could retrieve his personal voice greeting from it. On the way, I prayed that one of two guys would be there working. I knew these two and I only wanted to talk with them. When I walked around the corner at the store, I saw both of them standing there! One was working and the other just happened to be there on his day off.

I told them what I wanted and they both had such compassion in their eyes. As they shook their heads no, they explained how water would delete everything from this type of phone. It was in no way water resistant. They were truly sorry. While they were explaining this, one of them replaced the old battery and turned it on. It came on! They looked at each other with wide eyes.

I can still see that look in my mind. They were shocked. I said, "That is just another God thing." They agreed. Everything was still there: his pictures, his contacts, his texts, and all his latest calls. Later I heard they were telling that story at their churches. It was something that just never happened.

The pictures on his phone were mostly hunting and fishing pictures plus several we had taken of him the last three weeks of his life. He made twenty-eight calls that day, which was an unusually large number. Five of the calls were to me. The last call he made was at 5:33 p.m. The screen read "Home."

Loren was especially close to Gary and thought of him more as a brother than a cousin. When she was a freshman in High School, she wrote an English paper of her experience from the three-day search for Gary and her relationship with him. Her teacher recognized Loren's tender heart and impressed upon her to keep the paper forever.

Rhonda found a note her granddaughter, Kaylee, wrote several months after Gary's accident. She listed twenty-two things she loved about Gary. Later, the mother of one of Kaylee's friends found another note she had written in her daughter's backpack.

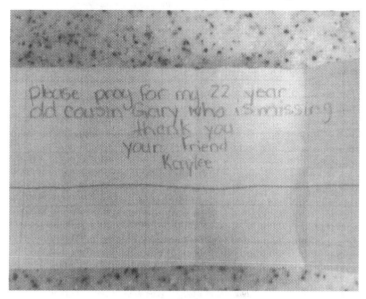

On April 27, 2011, tornadoes ripped through the South and devastated lives and homes. My sister's family home was demolished in Athens, Alabama. It appeared as though the tornado blasted right through the center of the house, taking belongings with it. Her family was in the master bedroom closet when it hit. They were uninjured, but devastated. They immediately ran to a neighbor's storm shelter and did not begin to survey their losses until later that night. However it would take the next morning's light to really see the awful extent of the destruction.

Everything in their foyer, dining room, and living room had flown out the back, taking walls and roof with it. Everything, that is, except for an antique chest in the foyer. My sister had the top of the chest covered with pictures of family and friends. The chest was the only thing that didn't move. Some of the pictures landed on the other side of the county from where they live. But there was one picture that did not move. Still sitting neatly, in its proper place, was a picture of Gary. My niece tried repeatedly to text a picture of this to me, but because cell service was down it would not go through.

It was obvious God had protected them. When we saw the picture, still in its place, we knew God had given yet another sign that He is always watching and He is always here. This was also a reminder that things can be replaced, but loved ones cannot.

The night the tornado destroyed my sister's home, a friend of ours, Brandi, had a dream about Gary. In her dream, someone was knocking on her front door. She opened the door to find Gary standing there smiling. (Having never met Gary, she only saw smiling pictures of him.) Gary said, "I was holding the hands of my family during the touchdown of the tornado." The dream was so vivid that when she woke up she looked out her front door … as if he might still be there.

It seems like God is always giving us little (or not so little) signs that comfort us. He lets us know that He is aware of our sorrow and loss and that He knows us intimately. These *God things* were designed especially for us, and when we were not expecting them. They involved other people as well as me alone. God can use anyone and anything at anytime. He chooses to speak to His very own.

Closing Thoughts

April 16, 2011
11:15 a.m.

On this day two years ago, at this very time, we were standing at our son's gravesite for his burial. My body was shaking uncontrollably from the inside out. In shock, I stood there not believing this was really happening. I heard our pastor reading the poem about a child loaned. On loan from God, Who has the right to take what He has loaned at any time.

Just last night for the first time, I heard a song about how God doesn't owe me anything. He has already done everything for me by taking my sins upon Himself and dying on the cross. "For God so loved the world that he gave his one and only Son, that whoever believes in him shall not perish but have eternal life."[1] This great promise of eternal life with the Father of all creation, His Son, Jesus, and all our believing loved ones is where I rest my hope.

> Our Creator will never cheat those of us of His creation who depend upon His Truth. And even more, our heavenly Father will never break His word to His own child.[2]

Being in relationship with our Creator, and knowing His promise of eternal life, is where we can rest our hope. God does not lie. His word is truth. We can be assured that we will be with our loved ones forever.

There are things I have learned and want to learn because of this loss. One is to know God more. When we think we have God and His ways figured out, He will come like never before and throw us off our way of thinking. I don't want to know Him more so I can figure this whole thing out and have all my questions answered, but I want to know what He wants me to do with what He has given. I want to grasp the best I am able, "How wide and long and high and deep is the love of Christ, and to know this love that surpasses knowledge."[3]

I want to keep in perspective what really matters in life. We are here for a purpose and that purpose Jesus spoke about as the greatest commandment: "Love the Lord your God with all your heart and with all your soul and with all your mind."[4] The next thing Jesus says is to love others as yourself. Sometimes these words are better understood through hardships, afflictions, and trials. When life is sweet and all goes our way, it is easy to say, *all is well*. However, when sorrows devastate our life, the *all is well* flows from the depths of our soul.

I want to live with compassion and to comfort those "in any trouble with the comfort we ourselves have received from God."[5] The comfort that others have given me, even though they may not have understood my grief, and the comfort from God who does understand, has given me strength and a grateful heart.

I want to comprehend that heaven is our real home and that is truly where our hearts and treasure should be. What the Lord plans for us in this life has eternal value and, when we realize this, our perspective changes. This life is so short compared to eternity. Eternity, where my faith will have sight and I will be with my son forever.

We don't yet see things clearly. We're squinting in a fog, peering through a mist. But it won't be long before the weather clears and the sun shines bright! We'll see it all then, see it all as clearly as God sees us, knowing him directly just as He knows us![6]

Gary Scott Lindsey
October 27, 1986–April 8, 2009

www.garylindsey.net

Notes

Preface
1. Isaiah 55:8.
2. John 14:19.
3. Taken from *Streams in the Desert* by L.B. Cowman Copyright ©1997 by Zondervan. Used by permission of Zondervan, www.zondervan.com.
4. Romans 8:32

Chapter 2 Extraordinary Champions
1. *A Child Loaned*, author unknown.

Chapter 3 Good Bye, My Son
1. *Good Bye, My Son*, Janet Lindsey.

Chapter 4 Letter to Gary's Friends
1. Psalm 139:16.
2. *Not by Accident*, Moody Publishers, © 1964, 2000 by Isabel Fleece. Used by permission.

Chapter 6 This Isn't Fair
1. John 16:33.
2. John 16:33.

Chapter 7 Suffering and Sorrow
1. Jeremiah 29:13.
2. Job 16:7.
3. Job 30:16b.
4. Job 26b-27.
5. *Hope for Each Day*, Billy Graham. Copyright © 2002 by Thomas Nelson Inc., Nashville, Tennessee. All rights reserved. Reprinted by permission.
6. Taken from *A Grace Disguised: Expanded Edition*. ByGerald L. Sittser, Copyright © 1995, 2004 by Gerald L. Sittser. Used by permission of Zondervan, www.zondervan.com.
7. *When Sorrow Comes*, taken from *When Day Is Done*, by Edgar Albert Guest. Copyright © 1921, The Reilly and Lee Co. Public domain.

Chapter 8 Contemplations from Job
1. Job 7:20b.
2. Job 9:12.
3. Job 23:13.
4. Job 42:2.
5. Taken from *Streams in the Desert*, by L. B. Cowman, Copyright © 1997 by Zondervan. Used by permission of Zondervan, www.zondervan.com.

Chapter 9 Who Are You, God?
1. Mark 10:32.
2. Taken from *My Utmost for His Highest* by Oswald Chambers. Copyright © 1935 by Dodd Mead & Co., renewed © 1963 by the Oswald Chambers Publications Assn., Ltd. Used by permission of Discovery House Publishers, Grand Rapid, Michigan. All rights reserved.

Chapter 11 The Cemetery
1. Psalm 56:8 (The Message).

Chapter 12 Grief Journey
1. 1 Timothy 4:10.

Chapter 13 Tested Faith
1. *Jesus Calling*, Sarah Young, Copyright © 2004, Thomas Nelson Inc., Nashville, Tennessee. All rights reserved. Reprinted by permission.
2. Psalm 31:15.
3. Taken from *My Utmost for His Highest* by Oswald Chambers, © 1935 by Dodd Mead & Co., renewed ©1963 by the Oswald Chambers Publications Assn., Ltd. Used by permission of Discovery House Publishers, Grand Rapid, Michigan. All rights reserved.
4. Psalm 73:26
5. 1 John 5:14-15
6. Taken from *Streams in the Desert* by L.B. Cowman, Copyright © 1997 by Zondervan. Used by permission of Zondervan, www.zondervan.com.
7. *Be Still My Soul*, by Jean Sibelius. Copyright © By Breitkopf & Härtel, Wiesbaden. Used by permission.

Chapter 14 A Different Way
1. *Jesus Calling*, by Sarah Young. Copyright © 2004 by Thomas Nelson Inc. Nashville, *Tennessee*. All rights reserved. Reprinted by permission.

Chapter 16 Jesus Goes Before
1. *Experiencing God, Day by Day.* Copyright © 1998, 2006 by Henry Blackaby and Richard Blackaby, All Rights Reserved. Reprinted and used by permission.

Chapter 17 Fishing in Heaven
1. Taken from *Streams in the Desert* by L. B. Cowman, Copyright
   © 1997 by Zondervan. Used by permission of Zondervan, www.
   zondervan.com.
2. Luke 23:43.

Chapter 19 Identity Crisis
1. Taken from *A Grace Disguised: Expanded Edition* by Gerald L.
   Sittser, Copyright © 1995, 2004 by Gerald L. Sittser. Used by
   permission of Zondervan, www.zondervan.com.

Chapter 23 God Is Able
1. Ecclesiastes 12:13 (The Message).
2. Ephesians 3:20.
3. Jude 24.
4. Hebrews 7:25.
5. Matthew 9:28.
6. 2 Timothy 1:12.
7. Romans 8:39.

Chapter 25 The God Things
1. *I Am Your Father, You Are My Son.* Copyright © 2009 by
   Christopher Seale. Used by permission.

Closing Thoughts
1. John 3:16.
2. Taken from *Streams in the Desert* by L.B. Cowman, Copyright ©
   1997, by Zondervan. Used by permission of Zondervan, www.
   zondervan.com.
3. Ephesians 3:18.
4. Matthew 22:37.
5. 2 Corinthians 1:4.
6. 1 Corinthians 13:12 (The Message).